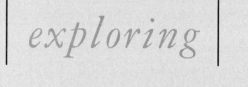

exploring

WEB DESIGN

Jeremy Vest

William Crowson

Shannon Pochran

THOMSON

DELMAR LEARNING ™

Australia Canada Mexico Singapore Spain United Kingdom United States

THOMSON

DELMAR LEARNING

Exploring Web Design
Jeremy Vest, William Crowson, and Shannon Pochran

Vice President, Technology and Trades SBU:
Alar Elken

Editorial Director:
Sandy Clark

Senior Acquisitions Editor:
James Gish

Development Editor:
Jaimie Wetzel

Editorial Assistant:
Niamh Matthews

Marketing Director:
Dave Garza

Channel Manager:
William Lawrensen

Marketing Coordinator:
Mark Pierro

Production Director:
Mary Ellen Black

Production Manager:
Larry Main

Production Editor:
Thomas Stover

Cover Design:
Steven Brower

Cover Image:
Chris Navetta

Cover Production:
David Arsenault

Library of Congress Cataloging-in-Publication Data:

ISBN: 1-4018-7838-5

NOTICE TO THE READER

table of contents

TABLE OF CONTENTS

v

exploring web design

table of contents

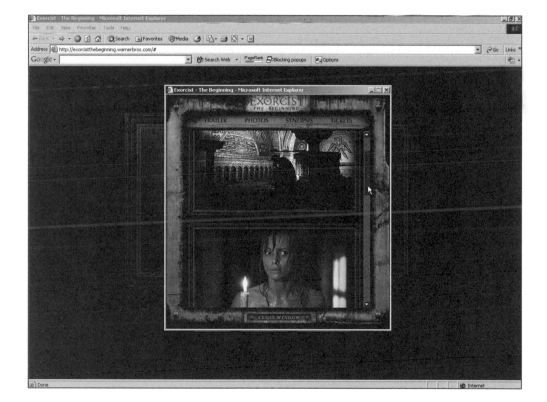

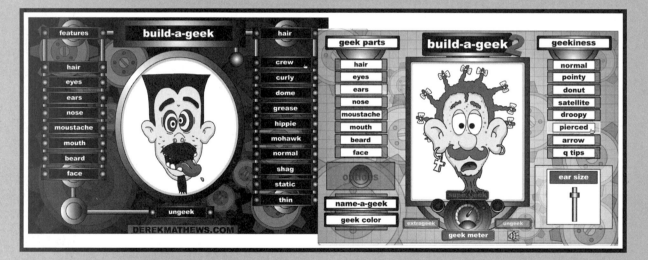

exploring web design

preface

INTENDED AUDIENCE

There are many books on the market today that teach the mechanics of website creation; some follow a specific software package and some focus mainly on coding and structure. While those things are very important, *Exploring Web Design* seeks instead to focus on the more elusive and sometimes subjective concept of design. In other words, this is not so much a "how to" book as a "why" book. It is about the big picture.

This book is intended both to help beginning web designers lay the correct foundation for a career in web design, and to help current web designers gain a better mastery of their skills through understanding. It presupposes a basic knowledge of the HTML structure of web pages, and some familiarity with image editing software.

BACKGROUND OF THIS TEXT

In a world where anyone can publish a website, the web design market is saturated with amateurs. Those who seek to pursue a career in web design must set themselves apart. That means not only acquiring and honing a wide variety of technical skills, but also knowing when, where, and how much to use them (not to mention, which ones to use). That seems like a lot to know, but it really comes down to one question: Why?

Any task performed without understanding is, at best, mindless repetition. If you understand why the task is being performed, you can optimize it, become more efficient, or even employ new methods to improve the results. This book is designed to clearly explain the reasons, and by doing so, open your mind to new possibilities.

TEXTBOOK ORGANIZATION

This book begins with an introduction to the overall concepts and ideas of web design as a whole. After that, each of the major components of design is broken down and analyzed in turn, beginning with the basic framework—the layout. The specifics of typography and color theory are discussed in their respective sections. Next, the reader is acquainted with the challenges and opportunities associated with making web designs that are accessible to everyone. Finally, the reader is invited to do some introspection, and discover those hidden creative influences. Special emphasis is given to methods of creative stimulation and expression, as the reader is encouraged to imagine and explore the new and exciting possibilities that arise from technological advances.

Chapter 1, *Make the World Wide Web a Better Place,* introduces the reader to the general ideas that will be dealt with in the rest of the book. An attempt is made to cultivate a certain open attitude regarding web design. The reader is encouraged to think beyond the superficial.

Chapter 2, *Successful Website Layout,* starts to explore the fundamental unit of web design—page layout. Design principles are introduced to serve as guidelines, and explained from a practical standpoint.

Chapter 3, *Web Typography,* explains why a seemingly mundane concept can be extremely important. The terminology and structure of typography are demystified, and readability and simplicity emerge as paramount.

Chapter 4, *Color Theory,* reveals the objective components of color. Artistic preferences aside, there are some basic rules that should be followed when choosing color combinations. This chapter explains why some colors work, some don't, and some are just a matter of preference.

Chapter 5, *Web Accessibility,* begins by suggesting that a good web designer considers the entire scope of the potential audience. The reader is informed about many common user disabilities, and the special accommodations that are required in order to access the Internet. Examples are given that show how to overcome design challenges, and helpful resources are suggested.

Chapter 6, *Turning Your Creative Potential into a Reality,* seeks to turn the designer's gaze inward in order to find that creative spark. Methods are suggested to fan the flames of inspiration, and advice is given about how to channel creativity into a daily workflow.

Chapter 7, *The Technologies of Multimedia and Web Design,* is about the future. A brief history of the technological evolution of the Internet is given, in order to suggest new possibilities. Readers are encouraged to begin to think outside the two-dimensional static interface, and to expand their creativity to new levels.

FEATURES

- Objectives clearly state the learning goals of each chapter.

- Photographs and illustrations supplement the text throughout.

- Text provides a valuable introduction to web design by focusing on the design concepts at work in all websites—layout, typography, color theory, and usability.

- Detailed illustrations provide a visual connection for design students.

- Real-life scenarios show how design concepts are put to work by professional website designers.

- Review questions and projects help to turn concepts into practice.

- Profiles of successful website designers offer important industry advice and inspiration.

- Articles by leading professionals in the field give valuable insight into the creative process.

E.RESOURCE

This guide on CD was developed to assist instructors in planning and implementing their instructional programs. It includes sample syllabi for using this book in either an 11- or 15-week semester. It also provides chapter review questions and answers, exercises, PowerPoint slides highlighting the main topics, and additional instructor resources.

ISBN: 1401878393

about the authors

Jeremy Vest

William Crowson

Shannon Pochran

ABOUT THE AUTHORS

With nearly seventy professional website designs to his credit, Jeremy Vest has a wealth of professional web design experience. Since 2001, he has taught ten different web design and design theory courses at Virginia College in Birmingham, Alabama. In addition, Jeremy serves as Art Director for Impact Advertising, overseeing graphic design and branding for the seven Virginia College campuses in the southeastern United States. Jeremy has also created a new graphic design program for Virginia College that began enrolling students in Fall 2004.

Jeremy graduated from Capella University in 2004 with a B.S. in Information Technology and a Specialization in Graphics and Multimedia. He has an Associate of Applied Science-Computer Aided Imaging and Animation degree and an Internet Webmaster Diploma from Virginia College. His certifications include the CIW (Certified Internet Webmaster) and the ACE (Adobe Certified Expert).

William Crowson is the assistant art director of Impact Advertising, as well as a writer and freelance web designer. He has been teaching computer graphics since 2002, covering subjects ranging from web design to multimedia and special effects. He has a Bachelor's degree in Philosophy and English, as well as an Associate of Applied Science in Computer Aided Imaging and Animation. His certifications include the CIW (Certified Internet Webmaster) and the ACE (Adobe Certified Expert).

Shannon Pochran is a writer and web designer. She earned her Internet Webmaster Certification and currently lives and works in Birmingham.

HOW TO USE
THIS TEXT

The following features can be found
throughout this book:

▶ Objectives

Learning objectives start off
each chapter. They describe
the competencies readers
should achieve upon understanding the chapter material.

▶ Sidebars and Notes

Sidebars and notes appear
throughout the text, offering
additional valuable information.

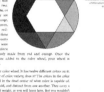

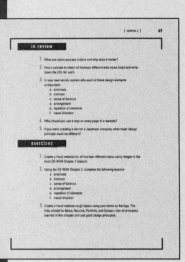

▶ Review Questions and Exercises

Review questions and exercises are located at the end of each chapter, to help the reader to assess their understanding of the chapter. Exercises are intended to reinforce chapter material through practical application.

▶ The Web Design Artist at Work

These career profiles are interspersed throughout the text. Each one features a successful web design artist in the field.

▶ Get Creative

It is important for anyone in an artistic field to understand the creative process. These articles are included to help readers learn how to tap into their creativity and get the creative juices flowing.

ACKNOWLEDGMENTS

Jeremy Vest would like to thank:

Foremost, my wife and daughter, dad, mom, brother, and Delmar for having faith in my dreams and me. Also, I could not have written this book without William and Shannon's amazing writing.

William Crowson would like to thank:

First and foremost, my wife Shana, for her invaluable love and support; my co-authors, Jeremy and Shannon, for their friendship and encouragement; and John M. Benson for being such a wonderful inspiration.

Shannon Pochran would like to thank:

My family and friends, especially my mother and Amanda, for all of their support.

Delmar Learning and the authors would also like to thank the following reviewers for their valuable suggestions and expertise:

Steve Campbell
A.I.T. Department
Lewis and Clark Community College
Godfrey, Illinois

Steve Bendy
Commercial Art Department
Des Moines Community College
Ankeuy, Iowa

Tim Jones
Computer Information Technology Department
International College
Naples, Florida

Bruce Huff
Visual Communications Department
Dakota County Technical College
Rosemont, Minnesota

Giraud Polite
Visual Communications Department
Brookhaven College
Farmers Branch, Texas

Gary D. Crossey
Media Arts Department
Blue Ridge Community College
Flat Rock, North Carolina

Chris Johnson
School of Communication
Northern Arizona University
Flagstaff, Arizona

Michael Davidson
Multimedia and Web Design Department
Art Institute of Washington
Arlington, Virginia

*Jeremy Vest, William Crowson,
and Shannon Pochran*

2004

QUESTIONS AND FEEDBACK

Delmar Learning and the authors welcome your questions and feedback. If you have suggestions that you think others would benefit from, please let us know and we will try to include them in the next edition.

To send us your questions and/or feedback, you can contact the publisher at:

Delmar Learning
Executive Woods
5 Maxwell Drive
Clifton Park, NY 12065
Attn: Graphic Arts Team
800-998-7498

Or the authors at:
Jeremy Vest: jvest@vc.edu
William Crowson: wcrowson@vc.edu
Shannon Pochran: shaeon@aol.com

make the world wide web a better place

CHAPTER 1

objectives

Develop a new perspective on the World Wide Web

Learn what makes a website good or bad and why

Discover how to apply objective rules to subjective matters

Begin to deconstruct the elements of a web page

introduction

Have you ever turned on the radio and heard a song that you immediately didn't like? If so, you probably switched to a new station after only a second or two and didn't think anymore about it. If someone were to ask why you didn't like that song, you might respond, "I just didn't." Well, when it comes to web design, that kind of answer is not good enough. If you're serious about designing web pages, then it's your job to make sure the fewest number of people "switch stations" after only a few seconds. To do that, you have to know more than just which web pages people like and which they don't. You have to know the reasons behind their preferences, even if they don't know themselves. You have to develop a new perspective, and that's what this chapter is all about.

DEVELOPING A NEW PERSPECTIVE

The World Wide Web is full of poorly designed web pages. The reason for this is simple: anyone can create a web page. Like a bathroom wall, the Web is there for anyone who wants to make a mark. And also like a bathroom wall, most of those marks are rarely worth looking at. There is a critical difference between the two, however. You're stuck with the bathroom wall, at least for a few minutes. On the World Wide Web, it only takes one click to find another website. That's where understanding basic design principles comes in handy. You have to make people *want* to see your web page. Now please understand, we are by no means trying to stifle your creativity. No one is saying that there is only one right way to design a web page. We're just saying you have to understand what people really want before you can give it to them.

figure | 1-1 |

This is an example of really bad web design.

Pictured here are some examples of web pages designed by people who never stopped to think about what potential visitors might want from their sites. Some of these pages use colors that clash so badly, it's almost painful to look at them. Others contain so many visual and textual

elements crowded together on the same page that it's hard to tell what's what. Still others, although they appear very attractive at first, fail to provide clear navigation, making it hard for visitors to find what they're looking for. If you want to succeed as a web designer, you must learn to avoid these mistakes and many others we'll discuss along the way. This book can help you. We'll point out potential blunders, explain what makes them so bad, and show you how to avoid them.

Critique to Learn

You've heard of learning something the hard way—making a mistake yourself and then having to fix it. Well, what's the easy way to learn? Watching *other* people make mistakes, of course. You can learn a lot from bad web design.

This isn't just a matter of learning what *not* to do, and then doing the opposite. Rather, the goal of this book is to teach you how to uncover the principles on which good design is based. Once you understand these principles, you can use them to create your own designs. That way, you're not just copying the good ones, but creating something original and developing your own unique style.

Keep in mind that when we say a design is bad, we aren't making fun of it. Not necessarily, anyway. We're simply saying that it doesn't follow good design principles, and therefore isn't likely to be a very successful design, especially if you're trying to convey a professional image. For example, if you're selling a product online, no one will want to buy from your site if it looks like a used car lot.

So what are these design principles we keep talking about? See for yourself. You're not just a potential web designer. You are also a Web user. You visit websites looking for information just like anyone else. Not long after you visit a site, you know whether you like it. This is as far as most Web users think. I like it—fine, I'll stay. I don't like it—click, goodbye. You have to do better than that. You have to ask yourself why.

Whenever you visit a website, pay attention to the things you like and don't like about it. Respond to the first thing that comes into your head. Remember, most visitors to your website are guided strictly by impulse, so learn to trust your own impulses. Then ask yourself why you had that impulse. Still don't understand what I mean? Ask yourself these questions:

figure | 1-2 |

Another example of bad design.

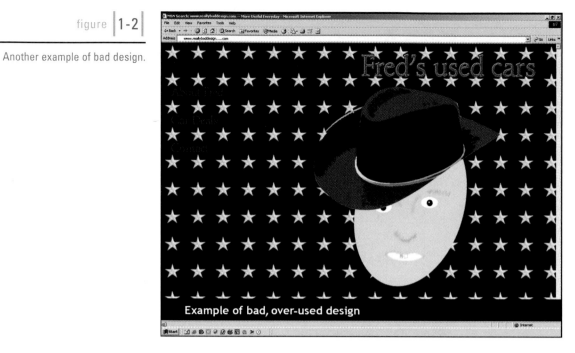

Example of bad, over-used design

- Do I like the way this site looks? Why or why not?
- Can I tell what the site is about? Why or why not?
- Does the design seem appropriate to what the site is about? Why or why not?
- Can I find what I'm looking for easily? Why or why not?

Look at the website in figure 1-3. Ask yourself the following questions about your reactions to it:

- Do I like the way this site looks? *Yes, it feels warm and inviting.*
- Can I tell what the site is about? *Not at first glance, but it is implied by the logo.*
- Does the design seem appropriate? *Yes, the design is classic and traditional, which is consistent with the way you would normally think of a bakery.*
- Can I find what I'm looking for easily? *Yes, the navigation is very simple and never changes.*

This may not seem like much, but these four simple questions can open up whole new worlds of ideas. You can also apply these to more than just websites. Look at advertisements in magazines, billboards, sale papers, book covers, even product labels. Each one of these was designed with a

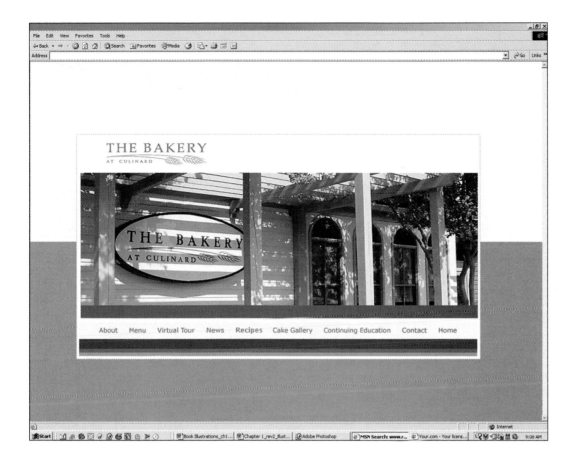

specific purpose in mind, and the design should reflect that. By asking yourself these questions, you can go beneath the surface of the design and begin to understand it. You can learn design principles from a *TV Guide* or even a can of peas. Your goal is to begin to see the lines, shapes, and color in everything around you.

figure | 1-3 |

Look at this website, and take note of your reactions to it.

You might think of criticism as a bad thing. The word *criticize* often means to bully or pick on someone, and therefore we think of it only in negative terms. Try to wipe that out of your mind. With websites, you want to use constructive criticism. You have probably heard this term before. With constructive criticism, the goal is to help you to learn, not to make you feel bad about yourself. It means recognizing the good things as good so that you can be sure to continue doing them. It also means recognizing the bad things as bad, but also looking for solutions to the problems they pose. Constructive criticism helps you to build yourself up, not tear yourself down. It can give you the insight you need to become a better designer.

Start to Critique Intelligently

Many of the answers to the "why" questions that you've come up with so far are only matters of opinion. Opinions alone may or may not be helpful, but are invaluable when backed up by design principles. Art is subjective, so even if you don't like the shapes or colors used on a website, it's not necessarily bad design. When you finish this book you will know the basics of design theory, and you will have the tools to view websites from an educated and critical point of view.

CONSIDER YOUR AUDIENCE

Anyone in the whole world can visit your site, but only those interested in the subject of your site are likely to. You identify those people—your target audience—and cater to them. Sometimes it's just common sense. For example, a website that advertises a product sold mostly to senior citizens shouldn't contain overly flashy graphics, small text, or hidden links that are difficult to locate. Conversely, a website that seeks to appeal to the teenage crowd shouldn't be too bland or boring. A website intended to sell you something online—a task that many people find frightening and risky—shouldn't look tacky and cheap. Other times, the

figure 1-4

Do you think this website is appropriate for its audience?

demographics will be more difficult to identify. In those cases, your clients may have to employ a marketing firm to do research, or they may have their own methods. Above all else, the audience is the main focus of design criticism. The design may be brilliant, but if it doesn't suit the audience, it won't get the job done.

What is Your Message?

The purpose of an advertisement or a website is to send you a message. Does the design of the site express that message effectively? Do you understand the message? How does the website express that message? This is very closely related to audience, but it's not exactly the same thing, as shown in figure 1-4. Designing for your audience means that your site uses colors and images that are more likely to appeal to your specific audience. Designing for your message means that your design focuses on and emphasizes the main message of the website. Confused? To put it more simply, if you design for your audience, the website looks like something your audience wants to see. If you also design for your message, you can tell instantly whether or not the website is for a restaurant, or a bookstore, or an auto dealer. If you put the two together, you are creating a more powerful design.

Expressing Yourself with Color

Color is a very powerful element of any web page. It can make you feel a certain way about a site even before you read a single line of text. Color is such an important tool that we have devoted an entire chapter to it, but don't wait until you get to that chapter to include color in your critiques. For now, concentrate on your own basic reaction to the colors. How do they make you feel? For example, the color red may convey a sense of intensity, urgency or danger, as in a stop sign. On the other hand, it can be provocative or tender, as with a heart on Valentine's Day. Do the colors clash or look wrong together? Are they appropriate to the audience, such as, are senior citizens going to react positively to alien green and orange?

How do you react to the color in this design? The biggest challenge involving color is to get past your personal preferences. Most of us love some colors and hate others. You have to divorce yourself from these preferences to really critique fairly. Just because the design is lima bean green doesn't necessarily mean it's bad design. If the colors are appropriate

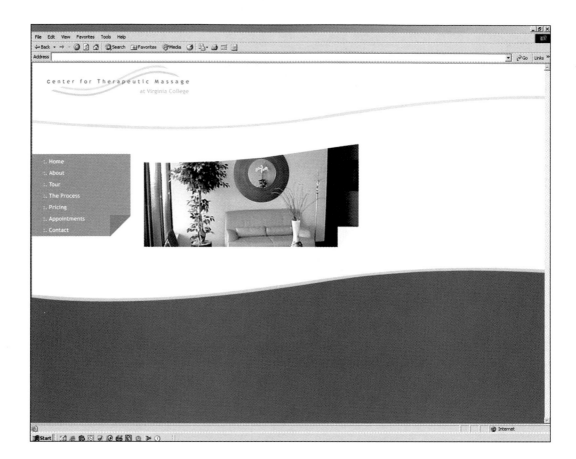

The balance of strong and muted, calming colors in this design suggests the essence of massage therapy.

and appealing to the audience, then it works. If you love bright, candy colors, you need to know that they are not appropriate for a bank website. If you love the bruise palette (blue, gray, black), you need to understand that these colors don't work for a site aimed at grade school kids.

Be Specific

When providing a critique, it's important to mention audience, message, and color, and be as detailed as you can. You should never tell someone that a web page is "too blue." What does that mean, anyway? The person receiving your critique could assume that you don't like the color blue. Provide details. Saying "I feel that using more colors would add to the design" is better than simply saying "It's too blue." Likewise, if you feel the message is not clear or that this design may not represent the target audience, you need to be able to back up that opinion!

Be a Good Sport

Did you really think you'd escape criticism? When you critique works with your fellow students, colleagues, or your friends on your favorite web forum, you should submit your work for their criticism, too. Remember that a good criticism is given to help you, and learn to accept it as useful advice. Don't be afraid to ask for more details. As you respond to their criticism, it's okay to discuss the reasons behind your design choices, but don't get defensive! Be open to what others have to say. If you plan to make a career in web design, you will need to learn to accept the input of others.

Just Design!

Is all this criticism making you nervous? Don't let it! The biggest killer of art is procrastination. Even if you're not sure if you are ready yet, start designing sites now! As you learn new elements of design, make use of what you learned. By the time you finish this book, you will be able to look back at your early site designs and see your progress.

GETTING TECHNICAL

A little girl was watching her mother prepare a roast for supper. Before she put the roast in the pan, she cut off both ends. When the little girl asked why, her mother said, "That's the way my mother always did it." Later that day the little girl called her grandmother and asked why she always cut both ends off her roast. She also said, "That's the way my mother always did it." Finally, the little girl called her great-grandmother and asked the same question. The elderly lady chuckled and said, "My pan was too small. I had to cut off both ends to make it fit."

Unless you understand the reasons behind the principles of design, you're apt to fall into rigid patterns that will hold you back. If you understand what the principles are based on, you can derive your own set of principles to fit any situation. Otherwise you'll spend a great deal of time trying to push square pegs into round holes. In this section, we'll get into some specifics about web pages, the images they use, and the browsers that we use to view them.

| **NOTE** |

Being a designer means putting your heart and soul into a project. If you can't take criticism well, your ego and heart will be crushed almost daily. However, you should also keep in mind that criticism is not always accurate. Sometimes it's simply one person's opinion, and other times it can be completely wrong. Never take criticism personally, and always temper it with your own thoughts and experience.

figure |1-6|

The RGB color model.

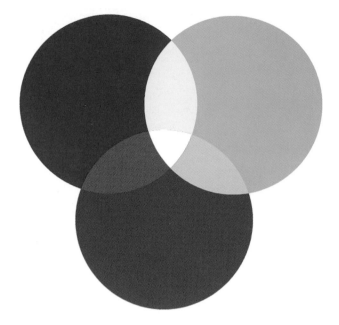

Basic Web Design Limitations

So now you are ready to design and the sky is the limit, right? Not exactly. There are some limitations you should be aware of when creating images for the Web. As we discuss these, you'll also learn some terminology that's common in digital art.

When working with digital art, you're actually working with combinations of red, green, and blue light (RGB). By mixing different intensities of these three colors of light, all other colors can be created (at least all the ones that can be shown on your monitor). Your monitor screen is made up of small squares that each contain three lights. Can you guess what color those little lights are? You got it: RGB. The colors produced in RGB do not include all the colors that can be seen by the human eye; therefore, not all colors can be seen on a computer screen. However, you will find that in most cases, RGB does a decent job, and it's likely that in web design, you'll never find RGB too limiting.

Raster Images

Remember those small squares with RGB lights inside them? Well, instead of saying "small squares," we usually call them **pixels**. Most of the images you'll use on a web page are made out of pixels. Any image that's made from pixels is called raster or bitmapped. The good thing about **raster images** is that each individual pixel can be a different color, so you can use them for images that contain wide ranges of colors, like photographs. The bad thing is, if you stretch or enlarge raster images too much, it becomes painfully obvious that they're made out of pixels. In other words, the bigger they get, the worse their quality will be.

each square is a pixel

After looking at figure 1-7, you should understand why it's usually not a good idea to enlarge raster images. You may not know how to do that right now. However, as you progress through this book and start to learn about things like HTML and graphic design software, you will discover ways to enlarge your raster images. Just remember: be careful when you do it!

figure |1-7|

Look at the magnified area, and you can see that the image is really made out of many tiny pixels.

But what about reducing the images? Obviously, as you shrink an image you lose detail since the whole image has become harder to see. Sometimes, this can actually help. Reducing it makes the flaws harder to see, so the image as a whole may look better, as long as it's done right. If the image is reduced proportionately (height and width reduced at the same ratio), then there's no problem. If one dimension is reduced more than the other, the image will look squashed from the top or the side. Consequently, it will look unprofessional. If you need to reduce a raster image, make sure you use professional graphic or photo editing software to make sure it's done right.

Speaking of graphic editing software, if you have scanned your photo or have created an image that you want to use on a website, it's important to use the correct resolution. **Resolution** is how many pixels per square inch that your image takes up. Whenever you save images for the Web, always use 72 pixels per inch, because monitors can only display between 72 and 96 pixels per inch. Your graphic editing software may refer to this as ppi (pixels per inch) or dpi (dots per inch). Dpi actually refers to the resolution of a printed item, but using 72 dpi will work the same for the Web as 72 ppi.

Vector Images

Remember when we said you shouldn't enlarge raster images? That's still true, but you can enlarge vector images all you want. A **vector image** is created not from pixels, but by connecting a line between dots. Before the computer draws a vector image on the screen, it calculates all its points and lines. If a vector image is doubled in size, the computer simply multiplies the positions of all those points by two, calculates new lines between them, and then redraws the double-sized image perfectly. There is no loss in quality. For this reason, vector images are said to be **resolution independent**.

Wow, that sounds great, but what's the catch? Here it is: since vector images aren't created from many tiny pixels, they can't have anything like the range of colors that's possible with a raster image.

So how do you know which type of image to use? Simple. Raster images have a wide range of color, but can't be enlarged. Use them for anything that needs a wide range of color but will always stay the same size, such as photographs. Vector images have a limited range of color, but can be resized whenever necessary. Use them for things like logos that include text and/or symbols and need to be different sizes in different contexts.

figure |1-8|

The original size of the logo is represented by the one in the middle. Both the left and right versions were enlarged to the same size; however, the one on the left was vector-based, while the one on the right was raster-based. Can you see the difference in quality?

> ## RASTER AND VECTOR: FURTHER CLARIFICATION
>
> Think of raster and vector in this way: if you have a yellow balloon, and you inflate it, the balloon is still yellow. The balloon was made with a flexible yellow material, and that material simply stretches. But let's say you want the balloon to be red. You paint it red with acrylic paint. As the balloon is blown up, the dried acrylic paint cracks. Try it! The acrylic paint will not stretch. Vector images are like the balloon, which stretches. Raster images are like the paint, which will not stretch.

Dithering

On the Web, you are working with a limited color palette, far more limited than RGB. The quality of your images will depend on the quality of the software and hardware being used by the person who is looking at your site. One of the results may be that your images will appear dithered to some viewers. **Dithering** basically means mixing colors you do have to simulate colors you don't have. Remember when you were a little kid with a box of crayons. You'd always lose at least one of them, and it always seemed to be the one you needed. You'd try to compensate by mixing colors that you had left. Like when you lost your orange crayon, you'd use your red one first, and then color over it with yellow. It never really looked as good as that orange crayon would have, did it? It sort of looked like orange, but you could still see streaks of red and yellow. Dithering is like that. It takes pixels of colors that your computer can display and places them close together, trying to simulate colors that your computer can't display. But why do some computers have colors that other computers don't? It all depends on your graphics card (a piece of hardware inside your computer that controls the graphics you see) and your monitor. If your computer has an 8-bit graphics card or monitor, only 256 colors will be visible. To put that in perspective, a 16-bit graphics card or monitor can display over 65,000 colors. A 24-bit graphics card or monitor can display over 16 million colors.

As seen in figure 1-9, images that use a large number of colors will have a grainy look to them on some parts of the image, especially in areas where there is a transition between colors. Most of your images that experience dithering will be photographs and complex graphics. There can be millions of different colors in a single photograph, and clearly a 256-color palette can't do any justice to that kind of image. Likewise, solid color line drawings use only a few colors, and look better on a computer with a lower quality graphics card or monitor.

figure |1-9|

Dithering is putting different colored pixels side-by-side to create the illusion of seeing one continuous blend of color. The image on the left is nondithered; the image on the right is dithered using a web-safe palette.

These days, even the inexpensive computers are very good, and most people have computers with more than an 8-bit graphics card, so it is not likely that you will have to limit yourself to the 256-color web-safe palette. However, if you are designing a site that is supposed to appeal to a variety of people, it's a good idea to keep the colors simple for those few people who still have an older computer.

Browser Limitations

As you probably know, a web browser is a program that translates data on the World Wide Web into a web page that you can see. Unfortunately, not everyone sees the same web page in the same way. This is because there are many different web browsers available, and not everybody uses the same one. Differences between browsers will probably frustrate you more than anything else when building a website. Every browser and browser version is different. A layout that is perfect on one browser can look terrible on another. While it is important to test a site on as many browsers as possible, we recommend that you design around the most popular ones. Trying to design for all the browsers out there is probably impossible and will only frustrate you, and most of the visitors to your site will be using the major ones. Keep up with browser trends and changes as well, because browsers are constantly being updated to meet users' needs. Not only that, but you never know when a previously unpopular browser may jump into the mainstream, or a currently popular one may fall into disuse.

File Formats for the Web

The most important feature of each of these file types is that they are relatively small. When you visit a web page, you want to see it as quickly as possible. The information it contains needs to be as readily available as if you had just opened a book. If your computer has to spend a long time downloading large images, it ruins the experience. It may also cause visitors to your site to get bored and leave. So it's very important to get the best results you can with the smallest file size possible (for more information on file sizes and download speed, see the table on page 145). To do that, you need to know which file formats to use for what purpose.

> ### ► FOR YOUR INFORMATION . . .
>
> JPEG stands for Joint Picture Experts Group, which is a subgroup of the ISO (International Standards Organization). They are responsible for developing standards for the digital compression of images.
>
> GIF stands for Graphics Interchange Format. It was originally created by CompuServe, but it was eventually discovered that the GIF format used compression technology that had been previously patented by Unisys, who now demands fees from software companies who use the technology.
>
> PNG stands for Portable Network Graphics. It was developed by an Internet committee specifically to be free of patents. It is intended to eventually replace GIF technology.

The following are the most common formats used on the Web, along with some characteristics to identify them:

JPEG

These are images with the suffix .jpg. JPEG images can contain up to 16.7 million colors, which makes it an ideal format for images that contain a wide range of colors, such as photographs. JPEGs are small because they use a compression technique called **lossy**. That means it permanently throws away small parts of the image each time it is saved, resulting in a loss of quality. The more data that is removed from the image, the smaller it gets. When you save an image into a JPEG format, you have control over how much data is thrown away. The idea is to find a good balance between quality and file size. In other words, throw away as much extra data as you can without making the image look bad.

- PRO: JPEGs can handle a lot of color information, and they discard unnecessary data to make the file smaller, so they're perfect for images with more than just a few colors.
- CON: JPEGs do permanently lose data, so your image will never look quite as good as the original. Also, this may seem strange, but JPEGs do not work well for images with a small number of colors. They tend to look somewhat grainy and noisy.

GIF

These are images with the suffix .gif. GIF images can contain up to 256 colors. This isn't much compared to the 16.7 million colors of a JPEG. However, GIF images don't need all those extra colors. That's how they stay small. GIF uses a method of color management called indexing. That means, it builds an organized list of all the necessary colors (anywhere from 2 to 256), and anytime it needs a color not on that list, it simply uses the closest thing it can find. So GIF is an ideal format for simple, solid color images and line drawings. Because GIFs don't use a lot of colors, they can employ **lossless compression**. This is the opposite of lossy. It means that once the colors are indexed, all the image data is left intact. Nothing is thrown away.

GIF also supports transparency (see figure 1-10), which is good if you have a logo that will be used on a variety of different pages but you don't want it to be rectangular. GIF also supports animation. By this, we just mean graphics that move, usually something very simple like a face with blinking eyes, or a mailbox with a door that opens and closes. You can create an animated image and save it as a .gif file; we'll talk more about animation in just a bit.

• PRO: GIFs use only the colors that are necessary without throwing away data, so they will perfectly preserve any image that uses a small number of colors. Since they support transparency, they can be used for creating images with nonrectangular shapes. They can also be used to display moving graphics.

figure |1-10|

The image on top has no transparency, while the image on the bottom does.

figure |1-11|

The top row is an example of the banding that can occur with GIF images. There simply aren't enough colors available to provide a good blending.

- CON: GIFs are not able to support complex images like JPEGs can. Making your GIF image more complex may also make the file size huge, and it will not look as good as the same image would as a JPEG, especially on computers with older graphics hardware. If you save an image with a gradient in a GIF format, banding will occur (see figure 1.11). **Banding** means that instead of a soft blending of colors, you get a harsh transition from one to another. The GIF format should only be used when saving simple, solid color images.

PNG

PNG may turn out to be the new GIF. PNG was originally developed to do the work of both a GIF and a JPEG. In fact, the World Wide Web Consortium approved PNG to replace GIF, and so officially, GIF is nonstandard at this time. However, not many web designers are creating PNG images. So, although PNG is the official standard, GIF is still used far more often.

- PRO: PNGs incorporate the best qualities of JPEGs and GIFs into one file format. They preserve good image quality, and support many colors and also transparency.

- CON: PNGs are not as widely used on the Web because historically they have not been as widely supported by web browsers as JPEGs or GIFs.

More About Animation

Our eyes are drawn to motion, so animated graphics naturally attract more attention than still images. You can make animated GIFs, or you can use web animation software to animate the entire site. Animation is lots of fun, but it takes up lots of space. An animated GIF is a much larger file than a GIF that is not animated. A fully animated website made with web animation software is basically a big interactive animated movie. That takes up a lot of file space, too.

Large files take a long time to load, and this can really work against you on the Web. Web surfers usually have a short attention span, and if a site takes too long to load, they'll leave it. Keeping people at your site is everything, so you don't want to bore or annoy the surfers. Use animation carefully. If the entire site is animated, keep it simple so that it doesn't take up too much space, and always include a loader. A **loader** is a small animation that comes up when users first access the site to let them know how much of the site has loaded. You might also want to make an animation-free version of the site for people with slow Internet connections.

Use care with GIF animations as well. People fall in love with animation, and want to put it all over the website. This is a beginner's mistake. Looking at a website with ten different GIF animations all going at once can be enough to make you dizzy. The site will look disorganized and busy. If you're putting a lot of animation in your website, ask yourself what purpose it serves. If it's moving, it will be the most eye-catching element on the page. Is that running teddy bear or that rotating @ symbol the most important thing on the page? If not, why is it animated?

CHAPTER SUMMARY

So, are you ready now? The more you study web design by evaluating websites, the more your own design skills will improve. As you critique, make sure you back up your criticisms by appealing to principles of design rather than opinion. Also, learn to take it as well as dish it out. Don't forget those design limitations we mentioned. Once you learn to work within these limitations, you'll find web design far less frustrating, and you may even enjoy the challenge of pushing the limits.

in review

1. List at least three questions you should ask yourself when critiquing a website.

2. What does it mean to use constructive criticism?

3. When critiquing a website, what are four important things to remember?

4. What is a pixel, and how is it related to RGB?

5. What are two major differences between raster and vector images?

6. What is happening to an image when it is dithered?

7. What is a web browser, and why is it important to stay informed about them?

8. What are the three most common file formats for the Web, and what is each one used for?

9. We know that animation is a powerful way to get attention, so how could including it in your web page be a bad thing?

exercises

1. Surf the Web and find five sites you really like. Study each site and write out a detailed list of the elements that attract you to this site.

2. Find five sites you don't like. Study each site and write out a detailed list of the elements that you could do without.

3. Design two fictional web sites: one for Grandpa Joe's Denture Cleaning Service, and one for Spike's Extreme Tattoos and Piercings. If you don't have access to web design software, or don't know how to use it, just sketch out your designs on paper and color them with colored pencils, markers, or even crayons. Think about how and why these two sites should be different.

4. Look at each of the sites you designed in exercise #3. Based on what you learned in this chapter, critique these designs. List the good points and bad points of each, and explain.

Logo

About | Cars | Contact

vc-tech

| successful website layout |

objectives

Learn how to design for the audience

Discover the different types of website layouts

Understand the fundamentals of web design

introduction

Ever try to make a website, and it just doesn't look as good as other sites you've seen? You know all the tricks the other guys do, you have all the same cool images, but it just doesn't seem to look right? Your problem may be the layout of your page. This chapter is all about learning the theory behind how the content and the interface are placed on a website. And it's not all just about making a pretty site, either. While creating a good website layout takes understanding basic design principals like balance and repetition, it also requires you to understand your client's needs. In addition to learning about page design and layout, you will also learn about designing for the audience. Essentially, you will learn the basic graphical layout concepts that you should apply to every website you create, and explore how to visually make a site a success.

WHAT ARE YOU GOING TO COMMUNICATE?

Before you start designing, there are a lot of things to consider. Who is this website for after all, you or your client? When you become a working web designer, you will be working for clients most of the time. In other words, you won't just be making sites for yourself or your friends. Obviously, if your client is paying you to make a site, you should know what the client wants to communicate. It's your job to understand the client's goals and the needs of the audience, and put all of this into an attractive and effective design. Sounds like a lot of work, doesn't it? It usually is, and if you don't have an understanding of the client and the audience, the web site will be ineffective.

Know Your Client's Needs and Success Criteria

Frequently, your client won't know what the website should accomplish. Most people think of a website as something cool and fun. That may be the reason why you are reading this book in the first place; you want to create cool things! Unfortunately, being cool is simply not enough, and frequently it will be your job to help your client understand this. You have to define the needs of the client.

For example, imagine you're building a website for a lending organization. They provide loans for middle to lower income families and individuals to assist them in purchasing their first home. Is it appropriate to put a video game on this site? Even a game that is similar to the theme of the site—like a first-person shooter that lets you blow away your debt obstacles—is out of place here; people are coming for financial help, not to play. Even if the client thinks games are cool and wants one on the site, it's best to advise against it, so that you don't compromise the professionalism of the company.

So perhaps at this point, when your client is excited about playing the "Debt Bloodbath Frenzy" game, it's time to start defining the purpose and goals of the website. The best way to get your client on track is to talk about the audience. Your client is in business, and a business person knows, more than anything, where the money is coming from. Once you and your client define the audience's needs, you should be able to map out the site with no problems.

Who Is the Audience?

Your client is probably seeking a certain type of audience, or already has a certain type of audience. Together, you and your client need to define that audience. You need to gather information on the audience's education, occupation, income, marital status, age, culture, gender, and so on. This information is called a demographic. **Demographics** are statistics that characterize your audience. The image that a demographic draws of your audience can tell you so much about how the site should look.

Put yourself back at the lending organization's site. The client tells you that the company's customers tend to be single women both with and without children, middle-aged married couples with two to four children, and elderly couples whose children no longer live with them. Your client has already told you that the customers tend to be middle to lower income. Based on this information, you can easily guess that this audience isn't the video games type. You can also see that these people come from a variety of backgrounds but have similar financial needs. What they will need on the lending website is information about the opportunities your client is offering them. Because of the varied backgrounds of the audience, simple is best. The information on the site should be clear and easy to access. Your links should be laid out in an obvious and predictable format, and there shouldn't be so many of them that it's hard to know where to go. Congratulations; you now know how to set up the links and content on the site! You've made your first decision on the design.

It may be that your client is still insistent on having something cool to play with on the site. Having defined the audience's needs, you can compromise. How about a mortgage calculator instead of a game? You'll probably have no trouble selling the client on this, because it keeps customers on the site while they calculate information for the house they want. This meets the audience's need, and therefore meets the client's needs as well. And remember, if you don't know your audience, your marketing effort will suffer.

What Technology Is the Audience Using?

What type of computers does your audience have? What size monitor are they viewing your website on? What is the processor speed? What browser are they using?

You may be wondering how you would know all that. While there are tools that can tell you what browser visitors to your site are using, they don't specify the speed and the monitor size. So, how do you know the specifics about what they are using?

Again, you use demographics. Frequently, you can make safe assumptions about your audience through demographics. If you're making a site for a gamer enthusiast magazine, you can probably pull out all the stops on the design: interactive animation, a huge design intended for a large monitor, downloadable movie files, and yes, even some of those coveted online games. That's because gamers will generally have the fastest computers with the biggest monitors; their computers will be able to handle the huge animation and video files on your site.

But what about our audience back at the lending site? We know who this audience is now: single moms, middle to low income families, elderly couples. It's probably safe to say that they're not visiting your site on a $5,000 high-speed gaming system. For this audience, the computer is probably being used to communicate through email, as a financial aid to help balance the household budget, and to seek useful information on the Web. Many people who use computers for practical reasons rather than entertainment will use a computer for as long as they can without updating it or replacing it. Some of them may not actually own a computer, but will use computers at libraries or at work.

Now, you should be careful not to stereotype your audience. It's possible that some of them do have very nice computers. But you can safely assume that many of them do not. Therefore, you don't want to design a site that will significantly inconvenience a large number of visitors to the site. Just as you need to design for what the audience wants, you also need to design for what technology they have. Because our lending site customers are frequently elderly, we're going to avoid using a tiny 8-point font that they can't see. Because many of them won't have a huge monitor, we're going to assume that some of them are still using an 800 x 600 resolution, which means that the site should be designed into a 760 x 420 area. Because they probably aren't using a high-speed Internet connection on a fast computer, we need to make sure the site loads quickly at low speeds. By understanding what your audience is using, you will be much more effective in the website's success.

Starting to Design

Now you know what the audience needs. Hopefully you and your client are talking about the customers and how great this site will be for them. Now you can define the site itself. You should create a site map for every website that you create, so that you can define how the site will look in a way that your client can understand and discuss it with you. A **site map** is a visual map of the site's navigation. Basically, it defines the links for each page, and where those links will lead. This is often referred to as website architecture, and for a good reason. The site map is the foundation your site is built on, like a frame on a house. If the architecture of the site is weak, the site will be weak.

You will also be ready to create a scope for the site at this time. The scope of the project defines what the client and the site designer will do, and for what amount of money. You'll learn more about the scope in Chapter 6.

THE IDEA BEHIND WEB LAYOUT

The last time you were at a website that was bad, did you think about why the site was bad? What made you come to the conclusion that you did not like the site? What is a website for?

| NOTE |

760 x 420 pixels is the standard size when you are designing most websites. Why? Because if your audience is using an 800 x 600 resolution on their monitor, a 760 x 420 site will take up the full page. The site itself is not 800 x 600 because the frames of the browser window take up some of those pixels.

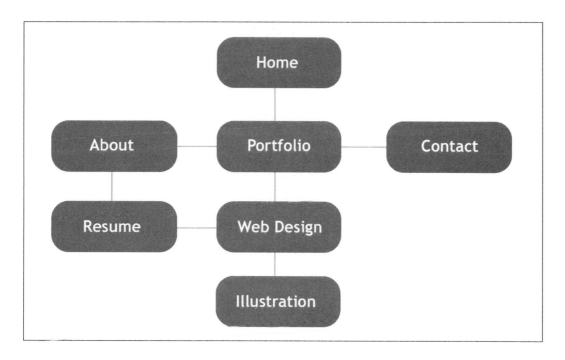

These are all very important questions to ask while looking at websites, including any website you may be creating. To help you answer these questions, consider what the site is supposed to do. Then if things aren't working out, it could be because it's not doing what it's supposed to do. You'll be better prepared to fix it if you know what is broken!

Most websites have one thing in common: the goal is to make money. Unless you're looking at a personal site, the site was created to make money in some way or another. If you are designing a site for a business, they are paying you to make the site for them. Keeping that in mind, I have never seen a company spend money and tell a designer "just put down whatever creative ideas you have for the website and don't worry about the content of the site." Some designers have a hard time accepting this, but the site is not all about the design. In fact, the opposite is true; the design is about the site, or at least about the content of the site. A website is for promoting, selling, and marketing. When you design your site, the design should enhance the content, not obscure it.

With this in mind, go to your favorite business website and look around. Does this site make you want to know more about the company and its products? Is this site easy to navigate and use? What makes the site easy to use? Consider these questions as you read the layout information below.

figure │2-1│

Site map example.

Different Types of Website Layouts

Why do most American websites look similar in navigation structure, logo placement, and design? Mostly, this has to do with something as simple as how we look at magazines and newspapers. Americans read left to right and top to bottom, so most of the time the rule is to place the most important element of the site first. That first element will also frequently be larger or will stand out, like a banner on a newspaper or the title of a magazine article. Some other cultures read right to left, and this will have an effect on the layout of their sites.

The second most important element will then come next on the page and will be somewhat smaller, but larger than or different from the main text. For example, designers often draw attention to the link menu by making the links bold, using a different color from the main text, or even putting them on or next to a small image.

However, you shouldn't always just stack the information from top to bottom. To keep websites looking interesting, web designers use a variety of different layouts. Below are just a few types of web design layouts. You can change between these layouts as you create different sites so that not everything you do looks exactly the same. I've used each of these, and they can all be successful if used well.

The Classic Inverted L Shape

As you can see from the image in figure 2-2, this site looks like an inverted L. This design is defined by the top and side bars, which are used for navigation and/or logo placement. This layout has been around for almost as long as websites have. It's like the invention of the wheel; when it was created, something easy and useful was born. Most people see this shape and know where to start looking for links. Unfortunately, the inverted L is so popular that it has been misused by nondesigners. You've probably seen quite a few poorly designed websites that use this layout. However, with the right design, it can be very effective. This is a great layout for corporate sites that should appeal to a large demographic.

Top Header

This one has also been around for a while. The top header, or top navigation, website typically has the navigation and/or logo at the top of the page. This keeps the page below the header free for content. In fact, I find that this design is one of the easiest to use when you want to make a website look simple, clean, and organized. This design is used often for **drop-down navigation**, as well. You've probably seen drop-down navigation before; it occurs when you mouse over or click on a link and a subnavigation menu appears. Adding drop-down navigation just makes this layout more organized, ensuring that the site remains clean and simple.

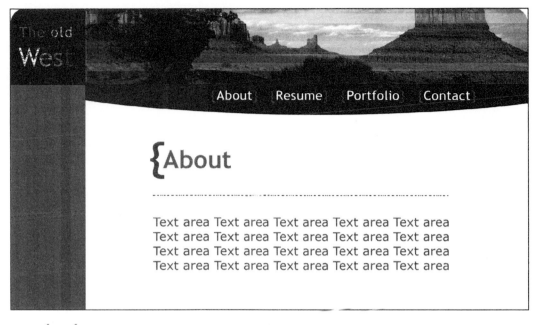

figure |2-2|

The classic inverted L shape layout.

figure |2-3|

The top header layout.

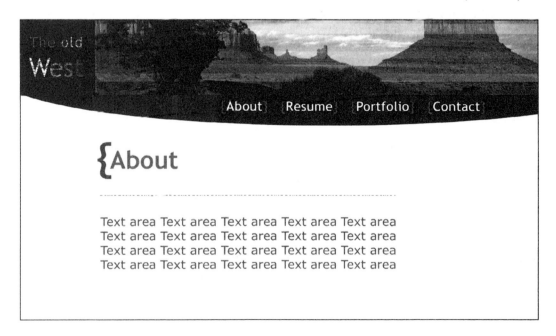

figure |2-4|

The side navigation layout.

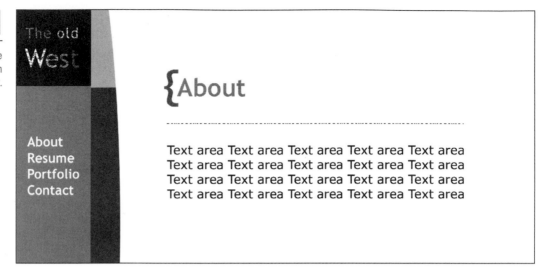

Side Navigation

The side navigation layout uses a sidebar only, with no top bar for the navigation. Sometimes designers will put the logo in the side navigation bar, or place it next to the sidebar at the top of the page. This design is also very clean. Like the top header navigation, it is very simple to use, and is used frequently by designers.

Box Shape

On this layout, all of the information on the site is in the middle of the page, inside of a square or rectangle. Sometimes you will see a very small element outside of the box, like a small version of the logo, but usually the entire interface is inside the box. The great thing about the

figure |2-5|

Box layout.

box layout is that it lets your eyes rest. You're not looking all over the sides of the site for information because everything is in the middle. Your focus is drawn to the middle of the page, and everything you need is there. This design is very effective, and has become quite popular as a result.

Classic Header, Content, and Footer

This layout stacks everything up neatly, from top to bottom. The logo goes at the top, the content resides in the middle, and the footer rests at the bottom. With this layout, you can put your links at the top with your logo, or at the bottom in the footer. The footer can also contain copyright and legal information. On some sites, you'll actually see links in both the header and the footer. The links in the header will generally be site links that take you to information regarding the products sold by the company, and the links in the footer will have information about the website, the corporation, and contact information. This is a very basic design style, and is a great way to organize information by importance.

figure |2-6|

Classic header, content, and footer layout.

Left Justified

When designing websites, you should design so that the site looks good at a number of different monitor resolutions. Frequently, sites are "stretchable," meaning that the visual elements don't stop at 760 x 420, but that the elements that exceed this space are not mandatory for the use of the site. Basically, these elements ensure that there is something to look at, regardless of the monitor resolution. This is good for people who have larger monitors with high resolutions, because it ensures that there won't be an area of empty space around the content when they view the site. Frequently, sites like this will be left justified. The left-justified layout simply means that the site interface and content are set against the left side of the page. If you want to stretch the site out, the layout can be justified to the left, and the content will remain there at a fixed size. However, a visual element of the site can stretch on endlessly to the right to maintain visual interest.

figure 2-7

Left-justified
layout.

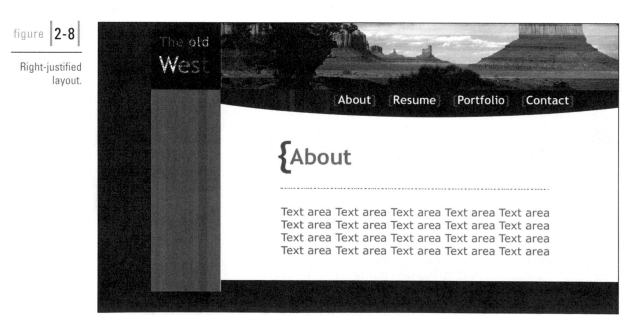

Right Justified

The right-justified layout is like the left-justified layout, only this layout is fixed to the right side of the page. No matter how far you stretch your browser window, this layout will stick to the right.

figure 2-8

Right-justified
layout.

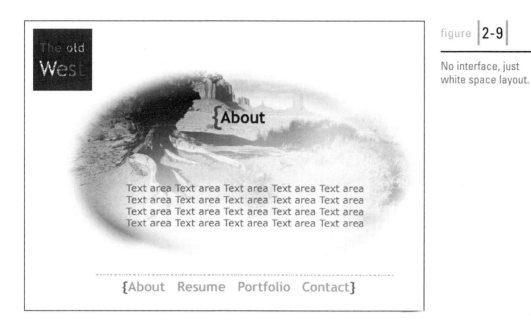

figure |2-9|

No interface, just
white space layout.

No Interface, Just White Space

The white space interface makes for beautiful and clean sites when done right. These sites have no drawn borders, no dividing lines, and no sense of interface at all. Elements float in the background, usually in the center, with simplicity and elegance. Remember that this type of page can be any color. White space is just another way of saying negative space, which just refers to all of the unoccupied areas on the page.

Full Design, No Room for White Space

This layout is the complete opposite of the no interface design. The full design of the site covers the entire browser window. These sites are defined by their eye-catching visual

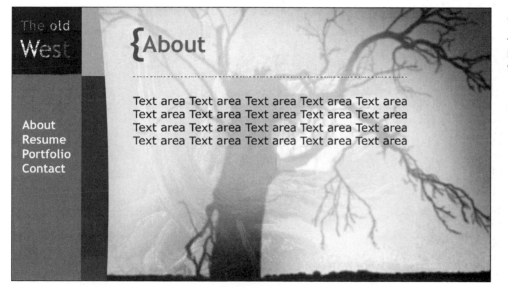

figure |2-10|

Full design, no room for
white space layout.

elements, which will frequently have a modern or futuristic look to them. The sheer volume of elements in this design results in an explosion of visual objects. Web designers are often attracted to the full design. What can I say; we love to see lots of cool looking stuff, and we admire the time it took to make something so intricate. This design has some clear drawbacks, however. It is very easy to make this design style simply too complicated, too busy. The audience may be so overwhelmed that they have no idea where to go. For this reason, this layout style must be handled with care. This type of design can be nice if done right or it can be too busy and confusing. If you use this style, it must only be for a business that this style of design fits, and be sure that it is easy to identify and understand the site navigation.

Middle Interface

A middle site layout puts the interface in the middle of the page, while the top and the bottom are completely empty. This is similar to the box design, only the middle site stretches out to the sides of the page, filling up the entire center. Like the box design, this draws the eyes nicely to the center of the page, and clarifies where all of the information will be.

figure |2-11|

Middle
interface
layout.

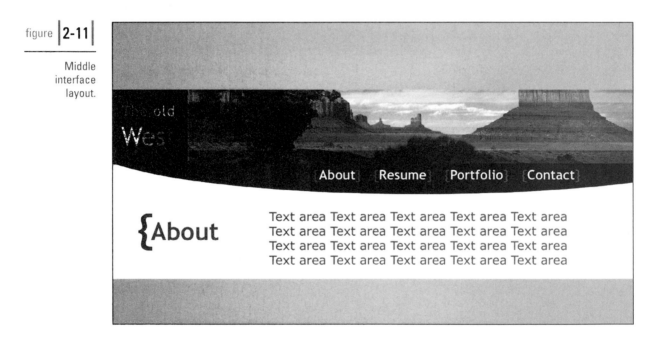

The Classic Black Site with Green or Red Text

This layout is nearly as old as the inverted L. As long as people have thought the Web was a cool place, they've tried to show us just *how* cool, with black backgrounds and blood red or alien green text. This particular color combination is almost never a good idea when it comes to business websites. It is well suited to sites for rock bands, sci-fi, video games, gothic sites, and personal sites. However, it should seldom, if ever, be used for professional sites. In all the

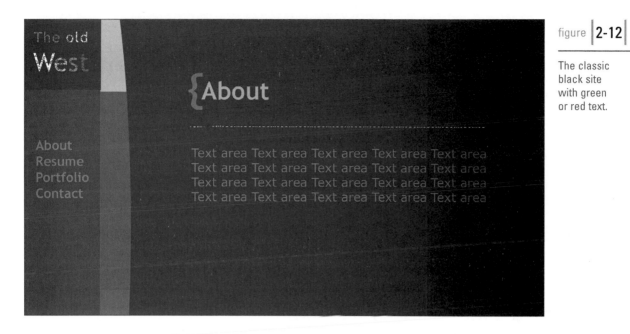

figure | 2-12 |

The classic
black site
with green
or red text.

years I have been surfing the Web and designing sites, I have only seen a handful of professional-looking sites with these colors.

3D Design

This layout is something you will see more of in the future. On a 3D website, elements of the site are created using 3D software. Sometimes, the entire site is designed in 3D. This design is a great break from the average flat site, and is becoming more and more popular. Unfortunately, the real drawback is download speed. 3D images and animations take a long time to load, and therefore these are not yet practical for sites used by a wide audience.

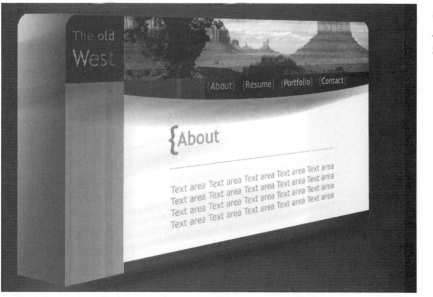

figure | 2-13 |

3D design.

Horizontal Scrolling

Photographers, artists, and online stores frequently use the horizontal scrolling layout to display their work or products. Instead of the standard site that scrolls up and down, this layout scrolls left to right. This provides a change of pace from the typical top to bottom navigation, but just be sure not to overdo it. Most viewers don't like to scroll very much, and scrolling to the right for several screens worth of information is pushing the limit of how much work visiting your site should be.

figure | 2-14 |

Horizontal scrolling.

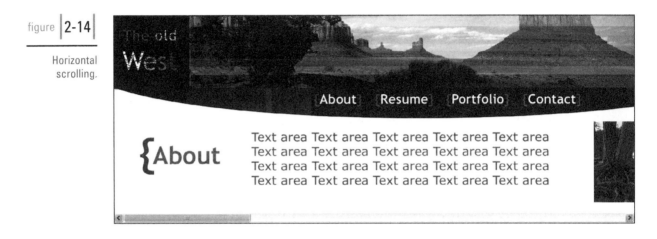

Unconventional Styles

Unconventional layouts adhere to no particular style. This doesn't mean there is no layout; when you see an unconventional site, it is usually clear that it has a very specific layout to it.

figure | 2-15 |

Unconventional styles.

However, they don't conform to any of the typical styles that you see on the Web. Art students, design firms, rock bands, and fashion designers create most unconventional websites. The inspiration for these is frequently drawn from everyday objects instead of from other websites or print designs. This category leaves you completely free to design whatever you like. It also gives you the greatest opportunity to fail, because you are using an untested design; you don't know how the audience might react to an unconventional site. As long as you make the navigation clear and easy to find, your unconventional design should be effective. Just be sure you're working with an audience that is willing to accept an unconventional site, and that the design meets the client's needs.

PRINCIPLES OF WEB DESIGN

Now that you know about all the different layouts, let's find out how to make those layouts work for you. Previously I pointed out that some of those layouts may not work if the design is weak. It's time to explore the principles of layout design so that you'll understand what makes a site good or bad.

Emphasis

Emphasis is all about what's important. The most important element on the page should be the most prominent, the second most important should be the next most prominent, and so on.

Why Use Emphasis?

Emphasis visually tells the website viewer what is important and makes surfing the site much easier with less confusion. For example, when I created the main headings for this book, I made them bold so the reader could tell the difference between the text and the heading. It also makes it easier for the reader to find certain text without having to read every single thing. Your website will emphasize things for the same reason. It will tell the audience what is important, it will separate the important stuff from the general content, and it will help the audience find what is important.

How Do You Know What Is Most Important?

Finding out what is most important on a website is a matter of knowing what your client wants to achieve. If the client sells shoes that already have a huge audience, the company logo should not take up half the page, but the shoes themselves might. However, if it is a new shoe company that is trying to establish a presence, the logo might take up a good portion of the page so that customers will remember the new company brand. The general rule for most companies is that either the products or the logo should be the most important part of the page, followed by the content or navigation.

When deciding what is most important, you should ask yourself these questions:

- What is the message you are trying to convey?
- What elements communicate that message best?
- Is there more than one message you are trying to present?
- What visual element is most appealing?
- Are there any elements that do not support your message and could be removed from the page?

Ways to Emphasize

Listed below are just a few ways to set the important elements apart from the other elements on the page. Remember, this isn't all there is, so be creative and explore new solutions.

- Bold
- Bigger
- Italics
- Different colors
- Effects like drop shadows, glows, and textures
- Different shapes
- Borders
- White space to set apart the other elements

The following figures show good and bad use of emphasis.

figure | 2-16 |

The logo is lost in this image because nothing is drawing your eye to it.

figure |2-17|

The logo is now one of the main elements of the page because the color and boldness draws attention.

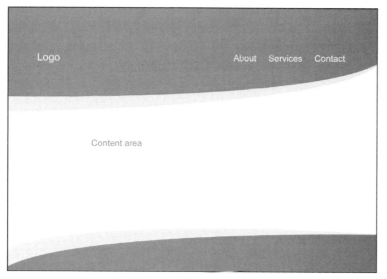

figure |2-18|

Again, the elements are boring, and nothing really pulls your eye toward what's most important.

figure |2-19|

By using bolding, color, and curved lines, the site now has elements that pop out from each other. What do you see first?

figure | 2-20 |

The body text is very plain and does not read well.

Objective

Seeking a position in computer arts that will

challenge me and allow me to utilize my

educational training, skills and potential.

figure | 2-21 |

The body text is now very easy to read because we emphasized the heading and separated the different elements.

Objective

Seeking a position in computer arts that will challenge me and allow me to utilize my educational training, skills and potential.

Contrast

Without difference or contrast, a website would be very boring. If the text, images, and logo were in the same color, font, and layout, it would not excite the viewer. Contrast is essential for generating interest. It also helps to guide the viewer's eye and makes the site easier to navigate. Using contrast is the easiest way to visually draw attention to a certain part of the page.

How Do You Know What to Contrast?

The logo, text, navigation, web colors, and images should all appear to belong in the site, but as separate elements. Anything that you want to set apart from the rest should contrast with the background and the elements around it. This is a great way to separate the content from the navigation, and the navigation from the links.

Ways to Contrast

Listed below are a few ways to get contrast from your elements. You may recognize some of these items from the emphasis list; that's because contrast is an essential element of emphasis.

- Reverse text (example: white text on black background)
- Larger size
- Italics
- Different colors
- Effects like drop shadows, glows, and textures
- Different shapes
- Borders
- White space to set apart the other elements

The following figures show good and bad uses of contrast.

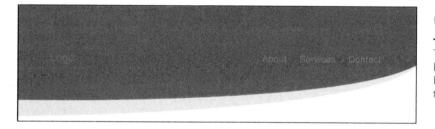

figure |2-22|

The logo and links are very hard to read because there is not enough difference between the background color and the text color.

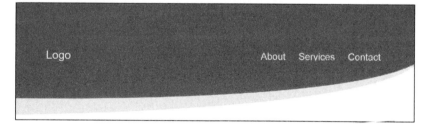

figure |2-23|

The logo and links are now very easy to read because the difference between the background and text color is greater.

Logo

About   Portfolio   Contact

Content area

figure |2-24|

This website is too plain and looks unorganized.

figure | 2-25 |

By adding contrast, the site
is split up into sections, which
gives it more organization.

Sense of Balance

The fine art of visual balance is something that takes time to develop. Some people are born with this sense and it comes naturally; others have to practice. Think of your web page as an item balancing on a point. In your mind, divide the site down the middle. Are there more items on the left than on the right? Or less? If this site was balancing on a point, which way would it tilt? Now divide it again, from side to side, so that the top and bottom are halved. Is everything crammed into the top of the site, or the bottom? To balance a site, the left and right, top and bottom must balance. This doesn't mean that your site must be perfectly symmetrical, so that you could fold it down the middle and see the same thing on each side. In fact, perfect symmetry is usually discouraged in web design. It simply means that the elements on the site shouldn't lean too heavily to one side. Make sure that the visual weight of the lines, images, color, shapes, and text of the site are all balanced. Remember that with the right use of color, a very small circle can carry as much visual weight as a large circle.

The Balancing Act

The following figures show websites that have no balance, and then what we did to create a balanced site.

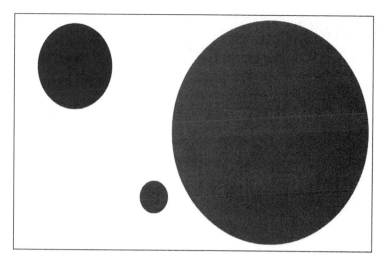

figure |2-26|

The circles are not balanced
because the visual weight of
the circle on the right is too big
to balance the other circles.

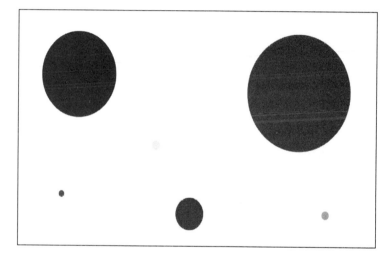

figure |2-27|

The circles are much more
visually balanced now.

figure |2-28|

This design has too much going
on in the left side of the page,
and the right side is almost
empty.

THE WEB DESIGN ARTIST AT WORK

Marc Silver

Job Title: Director of Market-Centered Design

Organization: Educational Testing Service (ETS)

Number of years in field: 25

Partial client list: McGraw Hill, Oxford University Press, Thomson Learning, Scott Foresman Addison Wesley, AT&T, Compaq

Professional affiliations: Special Interest Group in Computer-Human Interaction (SIGCHI) of the Association of Computing Machinery

Books authored: *Exploring Interface Design*, Thomson Delmar Learning

Magazines written for: *CBT (Computer-Based Training) Directions, Training Magazine*

Degrees/Certifications: B.S.

Awards: Codie Finalist Awards (4), Chicago Book Club Award, NJ Tech Award

Websites: Various websites and web applications for educational publishers, and corporations

What type of work do you do?

I am responsible for designing the user experience for websites, web applications, and multimedia software.

What got you interested in this field?

Working as a product consultant for Sperry Corp. in the 1980s, I created animated demonstration diskettes to show the features and benefits of the products I supported. The popularity of these small productions led me to believe in the power of the medium to train, entertain, inform, and connect to people.

What was your first industry-related job?

After taking a home self-study course in computers, I landed a job programming business applications. This was a couple of years before the introduction of the first IBM personal computers.

Where do you find creative inspiration?

I browse lots of websites to find creative ideas and to get inspiration. I sometimes tap into my competitive spirit to inspire new ideas. Brainstorming with one or two others can vastly increase the quality of ideas you develop. I also like to use creativity techniques to solve difficult problems or invent new things.

What has been your most challenging project?

I am currently working on redesigning a large (10,000-page) company website. It involves working with many different internal groups and outside vendors.

What advice would you give to students interested in pursuing a career in your field?

To succeed in the field of user experience design, you should be both analytical and creative. Being an excellent listener and a skilled writer are both requisite skills. I would suggest taking applicable courses, reading books on interface design to gain an understanding of the

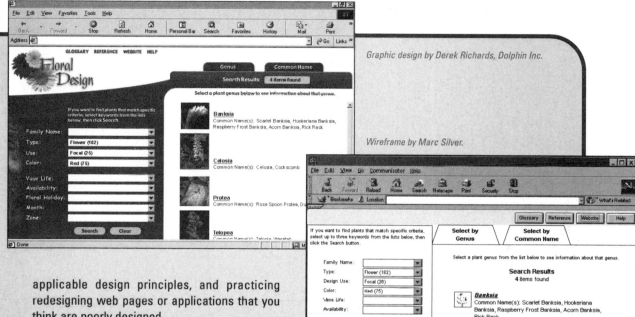

Graphic design by Derek Richards, Dolphin Inc.

Wireframe by Marc Silver.

applicable design principles, and practicing redesigning web pages or applications that you think are poorly designed.

What types of credentials are most important in finding a job in your field?

Most employers will want to see evidence of your skills. Use whatever contacts you have—family, friends, etc.—to find real-world opportunities to exercise your design skills. To gain experience, consider volunteering your services. If possible, shadow practicing designers to see how they accomplish their work.

What types of challenges do you face on a daily basis?

Besides the design challenges inherent in large-scale website design, we have to ferret out and resolve competing demands from different units within our company. Sometimes we have to make our internal clients understand that the end users' needs are of first importance.

How much of what you do is a collaborative effort, either between you and the client or between you and your co-workers?

Everything we do is a collaborative effort among interface designers, graphic designers, writers, content providers, web developers, usability testers, and others.

What are your personal/professional goals for the future?

I will always love designing interesting, challenging projects. I hope to become a more vocal proponent of excellent design and to provide design leadership to young designers.

How do you think your field will develop in the future, and how do you plan to adapt?

I believe there will be more and more emphasis on creating excellent user experiences in all forms of technology products. Bad design translates to unhappy customers, which hurts companies financially. More companies now recognize that good design benefits customer retention and satisfaction.

figure |2-29|

Do you see how much better the site looks after we changed and spread out the design elements?

Arrangement

The arrangement of the site is how the visual elements are connected to each other and how they lined up on the page. To make the site more harmonious, the visual elements must be arranged so that they align with each other.

The Importance of a Grid or Ruler

If you have visual elements that are close in proximity but not quite lined up, you should use a ruler or grid to make sure that the elements line up with each other perfectly. Being close is not good enough; if the items on the page are not lined up perfectly, the design will look messy. The following examples will illustrate this point.

figure |2-30|

This site is messy because the elements do not match up.

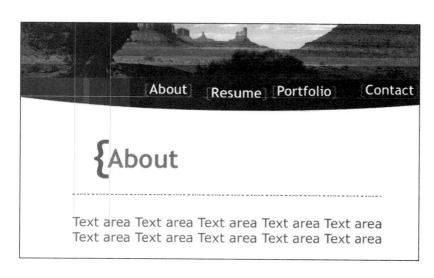

figure |2-31|

You can see how far off the elements are in alignment. Always use guides or a grid system rather than your eye to align elements.

Repetition of Elements

Repetition is the art of repeating elements, like colors, logos, and navigation placement. In web design, good repetition will bring up familiar images and colors repeatedly to maintain the theme of the site.

Why Use Repetition?

Think of a website as a very small software application. With any software, your users must learn how to get around the application with ease. If the navigation changed on every page, it would be very confusing. If all the colors changed on every page, you might not know if you're at the same site. If the logo is not on every page, how will the

figure |2-32|

Standard layout.

audience know where they are? The best way to keep a site simple and easy to use is to repeat the logo, navigation, and colors on every page. You will see some sites that successfully break these rules, but generally they maintain some repetition. For example, if the color changes on every page, the page layout will remain the same.

figure │ 2-33 │

Look what happens when we change the site navigation and design; it does not even look like the same site. It is recommended that you keep the navigation and logo the same on every page.

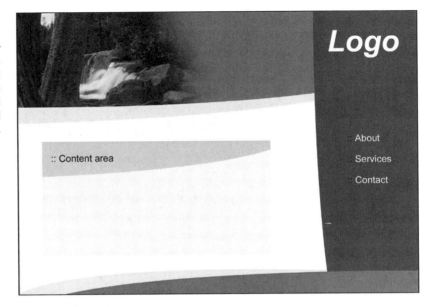

Visual Direction

Visual direction refers to the way the user's eye moves through the site. This is the direction in which you look at elements on the page, and it is very important that the eye moves around the page in a way that emphasizes the page the way that you want.

Why Worry about Visual Direction?

Visual direction helps guide the user's eye to the most important elements on the page. Without good visual direction, the site will not be easy to navigate. To see how this works, go to any website and see what element your eye goes to first, then see what your eye goes to next and so on. Make a rough sketch of the site using basic shapes, and draw a line starting at the first element your eyes see and go to the last—or just move your finger over the screen and visualize the path that the site leads you on. If the site leads a user's eye in straight sharp lines, the site does not flow well. I call a site that leads the users eye in straight and/or crossed lines an X or Z flow, because you feel like you are zig-zagging all over the place. A site that has more of an S or U flow line will be much easier on the eye, and will make the site easier to use.

Ways to Control Visual Direction

The visual direction of a page is something that can be planned in advance or created as you work. Either way, keeping the following ideas in mind will help you settle on visual elements that complement your site.

- When laying out emphasizing elements on the site, think how your eye will flow through the page.

- Cluster similar items together (example: all the text should be in a general area, all the navigation should be around the same place).

- As with emphasis, think about the visual message you're trying to communicate and have the most important elements lead your eye through the site.

- Be careful of arrows, pointing fingers, and curvy or sharp lines, because they may affect the visual direction of the site.

- The visual direction can also be affected by verbal elements on the page, like text and navigation. When designing, think of text as a piece of visual art.

figure | 2-34 |

A simple U flow site.

figure | 2-35 |

A bad, sharp line flow.

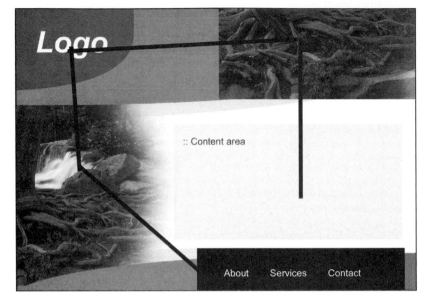

CHAPTER SUMMARY

You should now have a basic understanding of web design principles. It's up to you to practice, practice, and practice. And now that you understand these basic principles, you should start to critique every website you see and visually break down the basic design fundamentals. Study the bad sites as much as the good ones, so that you will know which mistakes you want to avoid.

in review

1. What are client success criteria and why does it matter?

2. Find a website to match all fourteen different web styles listed and write down the URL for each.

3. In your own words, explain why each of these design elements is important:
   a. emphasis
   b. contrast
   c. sense of balance
   d. arrangement
   e. repetition of elements
   f. visual direction

4. Why should you use a logo on every page of a website?

5. If you were creating a site for a Japanese company, what major design principle could be different?

exercises

1. Create a mock website for each of the fourteen different layout styles described on pages 26 though 35.

2. Create a mock website rough layout using your name as the logo. The links should be About, Resume, Portfolio, and Contact. Use all principles learned in this chapter and use good design principles.

web typography

objectives

Demonstrate the importance of typography in web design

Learn the best fonts for web print and why they are the best

Understand basic typography terms

Discover text as a graphic element

introduction

The goal of any web page is to communicate. Regardless of the theme, websites are a medium for providing information to an audience. Although a few websites are purely image-based, most websites rely heavily on text to communicate with the audience. When you work with text on a website that you are designing, it is good to know about typography. **Typography** is the manipulation of text on the page. Our goal as designers is to manipulate the text in such a way that it is pleasing to look at, and also expresses the message that is being conveyed.

WEB TYPOGRAPHY

WHY IS TYPOGRAPHY IMPORTANT?

Unless you have worked in graphic design for print media before, you may be wondering what typography has to do with design. After all, typography is just words, right? Perhaps you think that typography is not a designer's problem.

Wrong!

Typography is a very important element of design. The type of font you select has a huge effect on the message the visitor gets from your web page. Is this a corporate website? Does it have a friendly feel, or a cool, professional feel? Does this company have a fun attitude? Is this a radical, edgy website? The font can communicate all of these things. See figures 3-1, 3-2, and 3-3 for examples of what typography can communicate on a website.

When I say "font," what I mean is not the words themselves, but the way they look. A **font** is simply a style of printing letters, numbers, and characters. To a degree, your own handwriting is a font; after all, it is different from other handwriting, and recognizable as your own. Similarly, most fonts have a distinct look that separates them and makes them recognizable. Figure 3-4 demonstrates some examples of different styles of fonts.

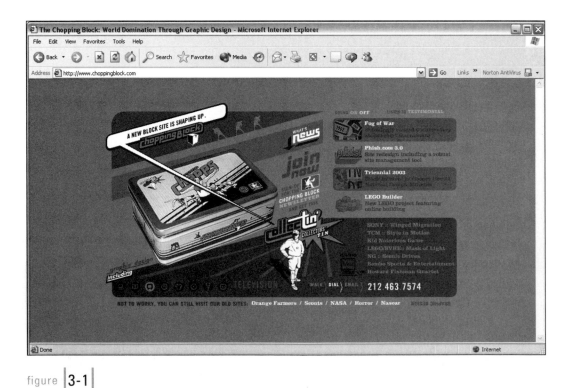

figure | 3-1 |

This site communicates a fun, playful feel through its fonts *(www.thechoppingblock.com)*.

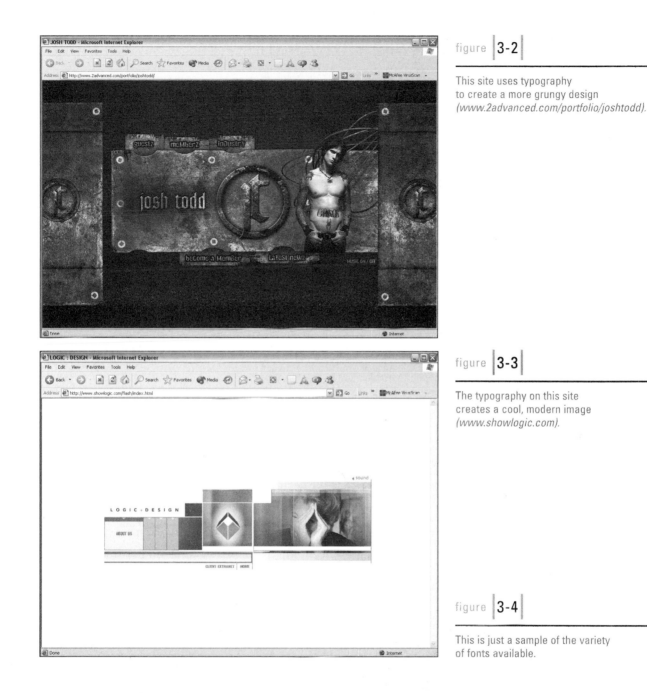

figure |3-2|

This site uses typography
to create a more grungy design
(www.2advanced.com/portfolio/joshtodd).

figure |3-3|

The typography on this site
creates a cool, modern image
(www.showlogic.com).

figure |3-4|

This is just a sample of the variety
of fonts available.

TYPOGRAPHY FOR THE WEB: CONTROL YOURSELF

So why do websites always seem to use the same fonts? If there are hundreds of thousands of fonts, why don't web designers use every single one of them?

Some try to, but there are very good reasons why this is a bad idea.

First of all, the Web has limitations. Every computer has some fonts loaded onto it, and it can only see the fonts it already has. Therefore, a web browser can only show fonts that are installed on that computer. If the font that you use is not installed on that computer, the viewer will instead see the default font that is used by the browser. Think of it like a tool box; if you don't have the exact screwdriver that you need in your tool box, you'll use the tool you have available. Perhaps you'll choose a screwdriver with a head that's slightly smaller but still fits, or maybe you'll just use the blade of your pocket knife. Your computer does the same thing. If the website specifies a font that it does not have, it will use what it has available. That cool site you made using the Moderne font will be viewed in the Times New Roman font by most visitors to your site. You can provide the viewer with a link to download the font so that they can view it as you designed it, but realistically, most viewers will not do this. Web surfers are interested in quick and easy information. Asking them to take the time to download a font and install it is usually asking too much.

This doesn't mean that you can't have a little variety. There are ten different fonts that are standard on almost all computers. The table below shows these fonts by category (table 3-1). Serif and sans serif are categories of fonts, but they are also two of the ten fonts, as most computers will include a font simply named serif and another simply named sans serif. You can rely on the user having most if not all of these.

table | 3-1 |

The ten basic fonts.

SERIF	SANS SERIF	MONOTYPE
Times New Roman	Arial	Corsiva
Georgia	Verdana	
Courier	Helvetica	
Serif	Geneva	
	Sans serif	

figure |3-5|

The ten basic fonts.

Be a Control Freak

Just in case a visitor does not have the font you prefer, you can recommend that they use the next best thing. The following HTML tag can be placed in the body of your document to ensure that you stay in control of the fonts:

*<font face="Verdana, Arial, Helvetica, sans serif">*Now enter all of your text between these two tags!*</font>*

The tag above will use the first font in the list that the user has. For example, if you were looking at my website and I used this tag, you would see everything in Verdana. If you didn't have Verdana, the font would default to Arial. If you didn't have Verdana or Arial, it would default to Helvetica . . . you see how it goes. Obviously, you can type the name of any font in place of Verdana, Arial and Helvetica, but it's always best to use at least one or two of the standard web fonts. By the way, it is standard to use only three or four possible choices when using this tag. You can load this tag with as many fonts as you want, but it's really not necessary. It would actually be unusual for a computer *not* to have one of the ten standard web fonts.

Easy Reading—Avoid the Headaches!

Although these ten fonts are standard, they are not all easy to read on the Web. Most of these were created for print, so it's no big surprise that they are easier to read in print. However, on a computer monitor, you are reading from an image that was created using points of light. The letters may touch one another, making it difficult for the eye to process the text. In print, you can control the size of the spaces between letters to make text more readable; however, this feature is not available using only HTML (although there are other options, which will be discussed later). Your eyes can get pretty sore if the font doesn't provide enough spacing between the letters. And the last thing you want is people leaving your site because it's giving them migraines, right?

figure | 3-6 |

Compare Arial and Verdana, Times New Roman and Georgia. You can easily see that Verdana and Georgia provide more spacing, which makes for easier reading.

This is Arial type.

This is Verdana.

This is Times New Roman.

This is Georgia.

Fortunately, new fonts have been developed specifically for web use. Thanks to font-maker Matthew Carter, we now have Georgia and Verdana, which have become the standards for web fonts. These fonts provide good spacing between the characters so that each letter is distinct and easily readable (figures 3-6 and 3-7).

figure | 3-7 |

This site uses Verdana for its main text. Even though they use Verdana at a small size, it is still easy to read (www.k10k.net).

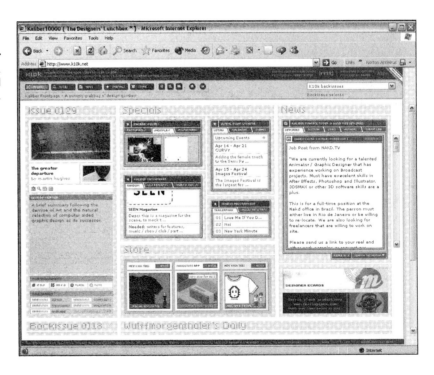

Easy reading isn't only about the font; it's also important to choose colors carefully. Certain color combinations do not provide enough contrast, and are difficult for the average person to read. For example, dark grey on black isn't the easiest thing to read. Usually if it's hard for someone with average eyesight to read, a color-blind person will not be able to read the text at all. Speaking of color blindness, some color combinations should be avoided completely so that the color blind can read the text on your site: yellow on green, green on red, red on green, blue on red, red on blue, and red on black (see figure 4-31 on page 94). Just think of how many websites you have seen that use red text on a black background!

figure **3-8**

At times you will want to use red and black, as they make a strong impact. In this example, the lettering is red. To make it more readable for the color blind, white was added around the text. See figure 4-31 for a color version of this figure.

For general reading, some color combinations clash, and have a glaring look to them that can cause eye strain very quickly (more information can be found about contrasting colors in Chapter 4). Keep in mind that the content on a website is intended for reading, and you should make it as easy as possible for visitors to your site to read it. This may mean sacrificing the theme you planned for your page, but in the end it's better to learn to use contrast to your advantage than to force the user to try to read neon green on neon orange.

This cannot be stressed enough. So many designers advance quickly in color theory and layout, and design some wonderful looking sites, but then lose it with the text. It's easy for a designer to get caught up in the look of a website, but people seek out websites for information. While it's nice if your site can be both attractive and readable, the user is seeking information and wants to find it quickly. The average web surfer will stick with the plain, easy to read site longer than the prettier, harder to read site. Good web design helps the user to find the information that they are seeking, and also provides an attractive, appropriate environment. Remember, in the end the goal is to design a website that allows people to actually find what they are looking for, and not feel that getting the information is a challenge. If the text is laid out perfectly, the user won't even have to think about it (figure 3-9).

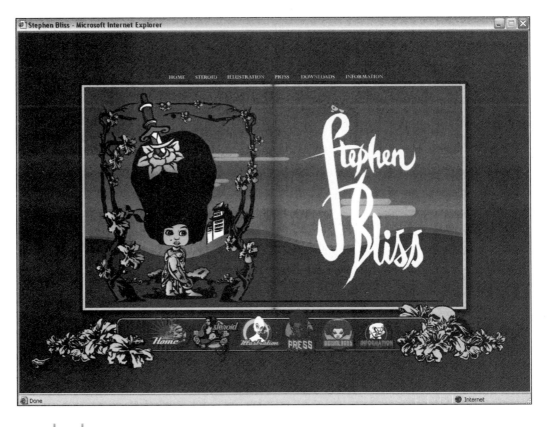

figure | 3-9 |

This site uses a great creative design, and the links at the bottom of the page are clear and easy to read. The designer also added the same links at the top in plain text to be sure that the navigation would be clear *(www.stephenbliss.com)*.

Some Words about Typography

When studying typography, it becomes necessary to know some of the terms commonly used in typography.

Font

Fonts are simply different types of text. If I write a sentence on a piece of paper, and then you write the same sentence and we compare them, our two handwriting styles will look distinctly different. We use the same letters, but the way the letters look will clearly be different, and each will be unique to the way we write. For example, maybe you write in cursive and I don't.

Maybe I cross the letter *t* higher than you do. Our two different handwriting styles are like two different fonts in this way. In fact, handwriting can be converted into a font for use on a computer. So fonts are simply the different ways that text can look (figure 3-10).

figure | 3-10 |

Notice the difference between the fonts used on this website (*www.hansliebschercopperwks.com*).

Font Family

A **font family** is basically a group of variations on a single font. These variations are also called *styles*. For example, fonts can be bold, italic, light, condensed, narrow, and so on. These fonts are not different enough to be separate fonts, and so they are all grouped together. Normally, when choosing a type of font from a font family, the font name will be pretty obvious. For example, in the Arial font family, you can choose from Arial Bold, Arial Narrow, Arial Light, and so on (figure 3-11).

figure | 3-11 |

Styles in the Arial font family.

X-Height

This is simply the height of the lowercase letter *x*. When fonts are created, the **x-height** is normally the standard for the height of the lowercase letters (figure 3-12). The line at the top of the x is called the *x-height line* or *mean line*, and the line that it rests on at the bottom is called the *baseline*.

figure | **3-12**

X-height, showing the baseline.

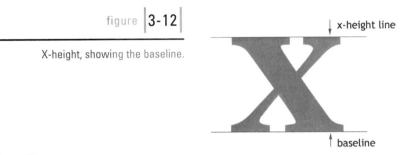

Baseline

The **baseline** is the line that the base, or the bottom, of the letters are aligned on. This is the line at the bottom of the x-height, as mentioned before. If you are writing in a notebook, you are most likely to use the blue lines as the baseline. Most of the letters rest on this line, although some letters have descenders, which hang below this line. For example, the lowercase letters *y, g, q,* and *p* all have a descender that hangs below the baseline.

In typography, you can set the *baseline shift*. This sets the text at a certain point above or below the baseline, and allows you to offset some of your text above or below most of the other words on the line (figure 3-13).

figure | **3-13**

Baseline shift. Notice how the *O* is lower than the other letters. It is below the baseline.

Ascenders

Ascenders are the parts of a font that go above the x-height line. The lowercase letters *b, d, f, h, k,* and *l* all have an ascender that goes above the x-height (figure 3-14).

figure | **3-14**

In this image, the ascender is the part of the *h* that exceeds the x-height.

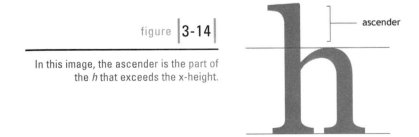

Leading

Leading is the vertical space between two lines of type. A higher amount of leading means that there is more space between the lines, which makes for easier readability when you have several lines of text. Lower leading means the lines are closer together, and leading can even be set low enough that the text overlaps, which can be used for a text effect (figure 3-15).

figure |3-15|

Notice the overlapping text in this image; this shows how leading can be used to design an interesting logo for a company.

In typography, the word leading is pronounced the same as *heading*. It dates back to the original printing presses when they had to use small pieces of lead to set the spaces between the type.

Kerning

Kerning is the space between individual letters. Kerning changes the spacing between letters in your text, and can be used to increase readability. It's important to note that kerning can only affect one letter at a time. Resetting the kerning is very time-consuming work, but you might use kerning to bring two letters closer together for an interesting text effect, as shown in figure 3-16.

figure |3-16|

The kerning was changed here to make the *O's* in the word "look" remind the viewer of a pair of eyes or glasses.

Tracking

Tracking is the spacing between all letters in a line. The difference between kerning and tracking is that kerning can only affect one letter at a time, whereas tracking can reset the spacing for all of the letters in an entire word, a group of words, or even your entire document all at once (figures 3-17 and 3-18).

figure |3-17|

This image shows a loose tracking, with plenty of space between the letters.

action/react design

5 5 5   5 0 th   w a y   s o .

p o t l u c k ,   n y   1 2 6 0 4

8   4 5 · 5 5 5 · 5 5 5 5

figure |3-18|

This image creates a fun visual effect with the word "accordion" by tightening the tracking.

the **accordion** brothers band

Scale

Scale is used to reset the height and width of your text. This doesn't change the spacing, but literally changes the length and width of the font. The vertical scale can be used to stretch or flatten the font up and down, and the horizontal scale can be used to pull or push the font left or right (figure 3-19).

figure |3-19|

The scale here is adjusted on the words "taffy co." with a taller scale, and the word "bayside" with a longer scale. This image would make a great logo for a taffy company.

Serif

The letters in **serif** fonts have tails at the ends of the strokes (figure 3-20). These are usually older, more traditional-looking fonts. While some serif fonts convey a playful tone, many of them convey a more serious tone (figure 3-21). In printing, serif fonts are generally considered easier to read, and are often the standard for newspapers and magazines.

figure **3-20**

A serif font, with some of the lines on the font clearly marked.

figure **3-21**

This site uses a serif font *(www.jiong.com).*

Sans Serif

Sans means without. So obviously, **sans serif** means without the tails at the ends of the strokes (figure 3-22). Sans-serif fonts are more recent in the history of printing, and frequently have a lighter, friendlier tone than the serif fonts. Sans serif is generally accepted as the easiest to read on the computer when reading several lines of text. This does not mean that you should not use serif fonts on your websites. On the contrary, serif fonts can make great headers and banners. However, when it comes to a paragraph of text, sans serif will generally be easier on the eye (figure 3-23).

figure | 3-22 |

The ever-clean
sans-serif font.

Sans Serif

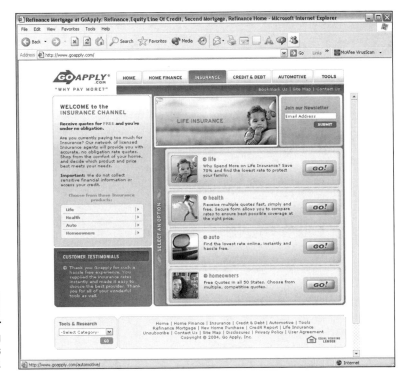

figure | 3-23 |

A site designed using
all sans-serif fonts
(www.goapply.com).

That's Great for Printing, but What about the Web?

As you probably figured out, most of these typography terms come
from printing. In some ways, they still apply mostly to printing, because
HTML does not allow you to set the kerning, tracking, scale, leading,
and baseline. You can still use these features in graphics editing
software, but with text, this method is used mostly for banners and
special text effects. You wouldn't use a graphics editing program to
write the bulk of your text, save it as an image, and then add it to the
center of your website.

So why have I spent so much time on this subject? Because of a
wonderful thing called CSS. **CSS**, or **Cascading Style Sheets**, allows you
to set a number of characteristics and effects to the text on your website.
Through CSS, you can set the baseline, the leading, and the tracking.
CSS also allows you to control the space between words.

THE ART OF CREATIVITY

robin landa

Robin Landa is an accomplished author of books on art and design. A professor at Kean University, Robin gives lectures around the country and has been interviewed extensively on the subjects of design, creativity, and art. She also serves as a creative consultant to major corporations.

Creativity seems mysterious. When I ask illustrious creative directors, art directors, designers, and copywriters how they come up with creative ideas, many claim that they don't know. Some say they don't think about a problem directly, but, rather, go off to take in a film or museum exhibit, and a solution seems to come to them in a state of relaxation. Other creatives are able to articulate something about their thinking process:

"I noticed how…"

"I saw that and thought of this."

"I heard someone say…"

"I thought, What if…"

After years of doing research into creative thinking—observing, teaching, designing, writing, formulating theories, and interviewing hundreds of creative professionals—I noted some fascinating commonalties among creative thinkers. What seems to distinguish a creative mind may seem, at first, unremarkable; however, upon further examination, one can see why the following markers can yield rich creative output.

BEING SHARP-EYED Part of almost any design or art education is learning to be an active viewer/seer. Whether you learn to draw a blind contour or observe the position of forms in space, you learn to be completely attentive to the visual world. Maintaining that state of alertness, of being a sharp-eyed observer, allows one to notice the inherent creative possibilities in any given situation. Being watchful when observing one's surroundings, everyday juxtapositions, allows one to see what others may miss or not even think is of note.

BEING RECEPTIVE If you've ever worked with or lived with a stubborn person, then you know the value of a person who is flexible, open to suggestions, other opinions, constructive criticism, and different schools of thought. Receptivity, as a marker of creativity, means more than being open to ideas. It means embracing the notion of incoming information and new ideas. Being flexible allows one to let go of dogmatic thinking, and to shift when necessary, to bend with the path of a blossoming idea.

COURAGE Having the courage to take risks is part of the creative spirit. For many, the fear of failure or appearing foolish inhibits risk-taking. Fear quashes that inner voice urging you to go out on a creative limb. Fearlessness coupled with intellectual curiosity, a desire to explore and be an adventurer, an interest in many things (not just one thing), rather than play it safe and comfortable, feeds creativity.

ASSOCIATIVE THINKING The ability to connect the outwardly unconnected feeds creative thinking. Bring two old things together to form a new combination. Merge two objects into a seamless different one. Creative people seem to be able to arrange associative hierarchies in ways that allow them to make connections that might seem remote to, or even elude, all others.

Creativity is truly a way of thinking, a way of examining the world and interacting with information and ideas. Whether you're designing a book jacket or taking a photograph doesn't matter. What matters is how you think about almost anything. When you are sharp-eyed, stay receptive, have courage, think associatively, and approach life with energy, then your work will be buoyed.

TYPOGRAPHY AS A GRAPHIC ELEMENT

There are hundreds of thousands of fonts available for use. What do we need with so many fonts? Fonts are a valuable design tool for expressing the tone of a website. Some fonts look distinctly happy or friendly (figure 3-24). Some lend a more serious and stern tone. Some fonts have a really cool cutting-edge feel to them (figure 3-25). Fonts can help to express what your website is about.

figure 3-24

The fonts on the Locks of Love website (www.locksoflove.org) add to the friendly look of the site.

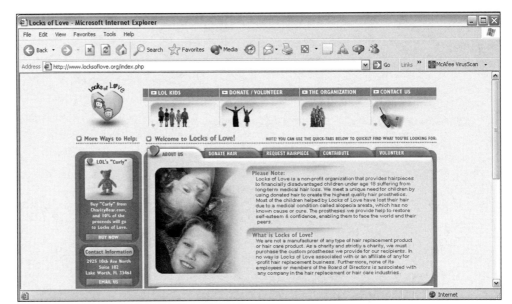

figure 3-25

Again sans serif is used, but the tall, narrow numbers and the minimal letters help to give this page a very modern and cutting-edge look (www.01-la.com).

I know what you're thinking. "You told us we can't use these fonts! You told us we are limited to the ten main fonts!" And for the main text of the site, that is true. But that is not all you are limited to in the graphics of the site.

That's where graphics design software comes into play.

You can use graphics design software to create text that adds interest and a specific tone to your site. Say you're designing a header for the top of the page; you create it using graphics design software, and then save it as a JPEG or a GIF file. It doesn't matter now if the users have that font on their computer; they will be able to see it because the computer will interpret the header as an image, not as a font (figure 3-26). You can also use this method to add special effects, such as drop shadows and bevel and emboss to your typography to make it more interesting (figure 3-27).

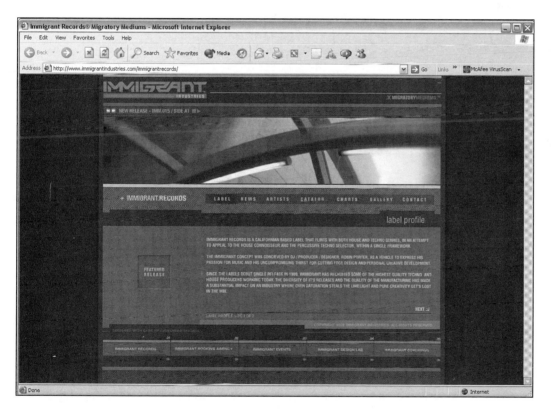

figure |3-26|

The font used on the word "immigrant" at the top of the Immigrant Records website *(www.immigrantindustries.com/immigrantrecords)* may not be in your font file on your computer, but it can be seen because it is an image rather than text written directly on the page.

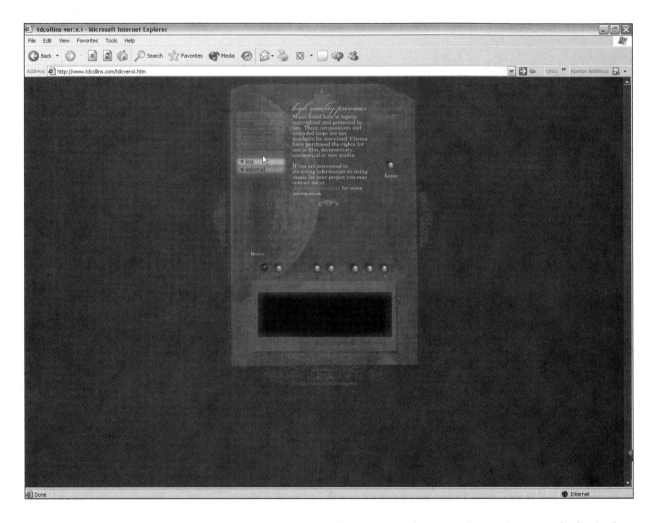

figure | 3-27 |

On this site, a glow is used behind the text to highlight the text on a hyperlink button *(www.tdcollins.com)*.

Using typography as an image is not only limited to headers; you can use letters as a background or incorporate them into the images on your site (figures 3-28 and 3-29). You can even use text alone to create a piece of art (figure 3-30). This type of image can convey a powerful message to the user, because it combines both the visual and the textual. The user can look at the font you chose, the way you used the text to make an image, and the colors you used to get an idea of what you're trying to express. In addition to that, you are using words, which add a more solid meaning to the artistic design.

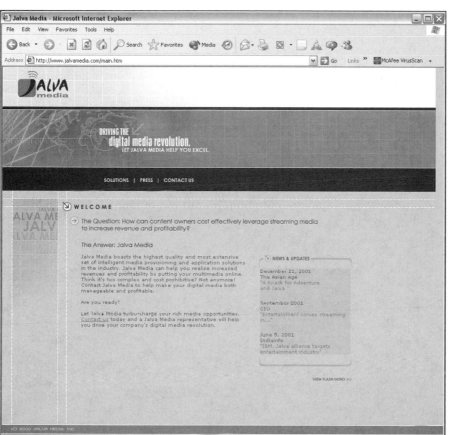

figure 3-28

This site uses text as an image in the header at the top of the page, but also uses text purely as a design element in the bar to the left of the main text body *(www.jalvamedia.com)*.

figure 3-29

This intro for a website uses typography as a graphic element in an animation *(www.createonline.co.uk/)*.

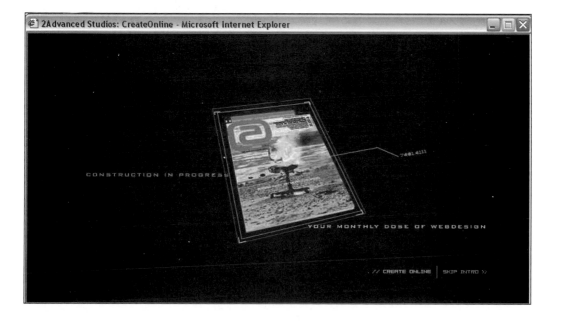

figure | 3-30 |

Believe it or not, this entire image was created using the letter *T* repeatedly.

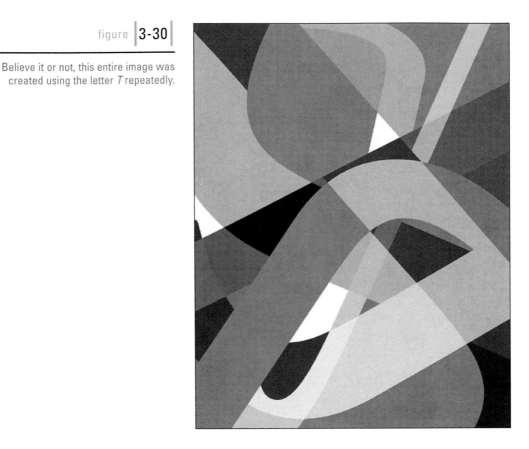

CHAPTER SUMMARY

At this point, you can see that typography is a very important element of design, affecting the way in which your website is received by the viewers. Typography truly can make or break your website. Finish these exercises to practice what you have learned.

in review

1. What are the ten standard fonts?

2. What HTML tag allows you to control which fonts are seen by the viewer on your site?

3. Which two fonts were developed specifically for web use?

4. What is a font family?

5. Define the following:
   a. x-height
   b. baseline
   c. ascenders
   d. descenders
   e. leading
   f. kerning
   g. tracking
   h. scale

6. What is the difference between serif and sans serif? Demonstrate by naming a serif font and a sans-serif font.

exercises

1. Design a new site or open up a site that you have already designed. Try out the ten main fonts on the text of the site. Notice how Georgia and Verdana differ from the other fonts. Choose the font that is easiest to read and best expresses the theme of your site.

2. Experiment with different color combinations. Choose a background color, and try to find the font color that is the easiest to read. Here's a tip: step away from the monitor and look at it from about three to five feet away. The colors should look good from that far away.

3. Design a header using graphics design software. Choose a word that is linked to certain ideas and emotions, and use a font that helps to convey this. In a critique, ask others to describe what the font suggests to them and compare it with your goals.

4. Make a typography image. You can choose a topic, or simply use your name, or even your first initial.

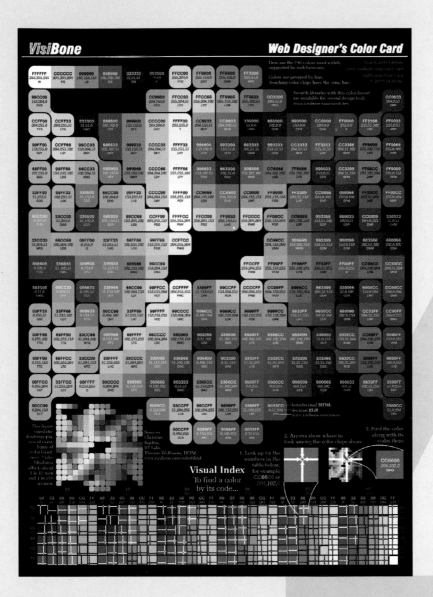

color theory

objectives

introduction

Color is very powerful; it can affect our moods and bias the opinion that we develop about a website. If used well, it can make a website into a beautiful and effective piece of design. But color can easily be misused, and can destroy a website in the process. For this reason, color is an essential part of the design process. It is important for you to learn how to use color effectively if you are going to be a web designer.

COLOR THEORY

BASIC PRINCIPLES

We all have some sort of experience combining and matching colors. It may have been coloring with crayons as a child, or sifting through paint swatches to choose a new color for your bedroom. Most people have a vague idea of how colors relate to each other, but as a designer, you need more than a vague idea. You need to understand color and be familiar with standard terminology so that you can discuss color intelligently with your clients.

Color Wheel

The color wheel is the most basic color lesson you will learn. In fact, if you took art in grade school or high school, you have probably heard of the color wheel, and relate it to ROY G. BIV (ROY G. BIV is the acronym for the colors of the spectrum, which are Red, Orange, Yellow, Green, Blue, Indigo, and Violet). You may have even made a color wheel in school. If so, good; your memory of this simple art project will help you out now.

The first three colors in the color wheel are red, yellow, and blue. These are normally represented as three points on a triangle (figure 4-1). These three colors are called the **primary colors**, because they can be mixed to create any other color.

If you played with finger paint as a kid, you probably know that you can mix the primaries together to make other colors. Red and yellow make orange, yellow and blue make green, blue and red make purple. The major colors that these mixtures make—orange, green, and purple—are the **secondary colors**. They add three more triangle points, so that now our color wheel has a six-pointed star in it (figure 4-2).

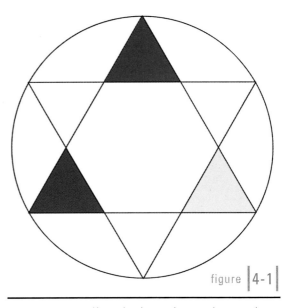

figure |4-1|

Here, the three primary colors are shown as three triangles in a star.

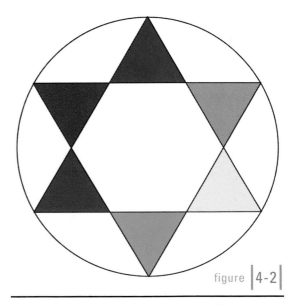

figure |4-2|

The three secondary colors are combinations of the primaries. For this reason, they appear between the primaries on the color wheel.

If you mix the primary colors with the secondary colors that are next to them, you get colors that fall in between the two. These are **intermediate**, or tertiary, colors. They are red-orange, yellow-orange, yellow-green, blue-green, blue-purple, and red-purple. The names of these colors make it pretty obvious what colors were mixed to make the colors;

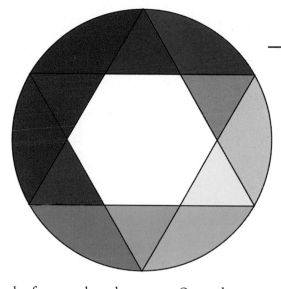

figure |4-3|

Our circle is complete! The intermediate colors are made of combinations of primary and secondary colors.

red-orange is obviously made from red and orange. Once the intermediate colors are added to the color wheel, your wheel is complete (figure 4-3).

Now, take a look at our color wheel. It has twelve different colors on it. Doesn't seem like a lot of color variety, does it? The colors in the color wheel pretty much fall in the dead center of what color is capable of. They are bright and bold, and distinct from one another. They carry a great deal of emotional weight, as you will learn later. But you wouldn't want to be limited to just twelve colors, would you? Consider the colors of the sky, of various flowers, of your favorite shirt. These colors are not fully represented within this color wheel, and all of these colors can have an emotional meaning to you. While these twelve colors in the color wheel make a bold statement, most designers want more variety so that they can express a broader range of emotions. Fortunately, you can change the values of these colors to achieve a greater variety.

Color Values: Tints and Shades

Value means lightness. Value is how light the color is, specifically when you compare it with your general idea of what the standard for a color is.

For example, look at the red on the color wheel. This represents the primary color red, which is the true red. This means it has no yellow or blue value, just red (see Note). If a red is lighter than this red, we call it a lighter value. The lighter values are called **tints**. If a red is darker than this red, we call it a darker value. The darker values are called **shades**.

NOTE

Just so you know, defining what is a true red (or true blue, yellow, green, or any of the other colors of the color wheel) can be tricky. It can be very difficult to define what makes this a "true red," or even if true red is the right thing to call it. But for the sake of this lesson, the red on our color wheel can be called true red.

figure **4-4**

The colors are shown left to right, with the tints at the top and the shades at the bottom.

figure **4-5**

Here is a cross section of the green from figure 4-4. The tint is on the top and the shade is on the bottom. Clearly, the top area gets lighter, and eventually becomes white. Likewise, the bottom area gets darker until it becomes black.

figure **4-6**

Tints and shades can only be different values of the same color. If other colors are involved (like the blue and yellow in this example), they are not tints or shades of the color!

figure **4-7**

Here, the green at the top is very vivid and bright. Closer to the bottom, it becomes less vivid, and finally turns gray. The green at the top is more saturated, and the green near the bottom is more desaturated. The gray is completely desaturated.

It's important to note that a tint or shade is a lighter or darker value of the color. In figure 4-4, you see the colors of the color wheel laid out left to right, and the values are given from top to bottom, with tint at the top and shade at the bottom. If you cut a sample of the green from top to bottom, you get the tint and shades of green (figure 4-5). If you cut it left to right, you can argue that the yellow is lighter and the blue is darker than the green (figure 4-6). However, these are not tints and shades. The tint and shade are the lighter or darker values of the color you started with. It is not the color made lighter or darker through the addition of other colors.

Saturation and Desaturation

We can define **saturation** as how vivid or dull a color is. The more saturated a color becomes, the more vivid and intense it is. A fully saturated color can be almost fluorescent. As you desaturate a color, it gets more and more dull—closer to gray. This is not the same thing as tinting or shading the color. Saturating a color doesn't lighten it, but adds *more* of the color. Desaturating a color doesn't darken it, but takes away some of the color (figure 4-7).

Values and saturation are important because this is how we produce the colors we see in real life. When you look around the room, you don't see everything in bright primary or secondary colors. You see millions of variations of these colors. Value and saturation are where these variations come from.

RYB VS. RGB

We've told you that the color wheel is based on three primary colors: red, yellow, and blue. This is called the **RYB** (Red, Yellow, Blue) **color model**. This is probably the way you've grown up thinking about colors. If you mix red and yellow, you get orange. If you mix red and blue, you get purple, and so on. However, when you deal with digital colors, it doesn't work that way. You may be asking yourself, why did you tell me something that isn't true? Well, it *is* true for all practical, *nondigital* purposes.

Color works like the sensation of taste. The way you see color isn't exactly the same way someone else sees color. We all see *basically* the same thing, just like we all agree that a certain food is sweet or sour. It's when we try to get too precise that things get difficult. So, we all agree that when you mix red (a broad category of color) and yellow (another broad category of color), you get orange (another broad category of color). We can also agree that certain colors work well together, and certain colors don't. Do tuna fish and vanilla ice cream go together? How about bananas and peanut butter? Most, if not all, people will agree that the first combination never belongs together. However, you will find a healthy disagreement about the second. Do you see my point?

Let's mix it up even further. When dealing with inks, paints, crayons or whatever, no two that are labeled *orange* are ever going to be the exact same color. Even two orange crayons produced by the same company, in the same factory, on the same day will be slightly different. The mixture of chemicals might not be exactly the same, the humidity at different times of the day may have caused the chemicals to interact differently, etc. On top of all this, there is another complication: colors that come straight from a light source (such as a television, computer monitor, or the sun) work differently than colors that come from light bouncing off other objects (for example: the carpet, your shoes, or your cat). We don't have the space to deal with the whys of that subject here, but you can find the answer with a little research.

Now that you understand that our perception of colors is not exact, I hope you also understand why we usually use the RYB color model. It's just that talking about mixing red, yellow, and blue to get all other colors appears to work well most of the time. It works so well, in fact, that the RYB model is what we used to create the standard color wheel.

Now comes digital color. Imagine if a computer could taste a certain food and numerically quantify the exact amount of sweetness, sourness, and a hundred other similar properties and record the interaction between them. Maybe one day a computer will, but our own taste buds just aren't sharp enough. In the same way, our eyes aren't sharp enough to quantify the exact frequency and interaction of the light waves responsible for our perception of color. But a computer can. The computer knows exactly how much light and which frequencies of light waves go into making a particular color. This changes all the rules. We've moved from "taking our best guess" to dealing with exact colors. Not only that, but we are dealing with exact colors directly from a light source—the computer monitor.

So how does this change the rules? Digital color uses different primary colors. Instead of red, yellow, and blue (RYB), it uses red, green, and blue (RGB). When you use graphics applications to design web graphics, you will notice that they are based on the **RGB color model** instead of RYB. Most graphics applications will simply allow you to pick a premixed color from a list (called a *color swatch*). However, if you ever want to custom-mix colors digitally, it becomes important to understand that red and yellow don't make orange anymore.

COLOR SCHEMES

So, what good is a color wheel, really? The color wheel can be used to help you determine color combinations. While we always encourage you to go with your feelings (and hopefully your eyes!) when combining colors, there are certain color schemes that work well together, and that many designers rely on.

Monochromatic

This scheme is simple. *Mono* means one, *chroma* means color. Therefore, a **monochromatic** color scheme uses only one color. This sounds pretty dull, but you can do some interesting things with it. That's because in monochromatic design, you are still able to use all the tints and shades of the color you select. While it seems limiting, working within the limits of a monochromatic color scheme encourages you to get creative with other aspects of the design (figures 4-8, 4-9, and 4-10).

Analogous

The **analogous** color scheme is very similar to the monochromatic scheme; however, instead of using tints and shades of one color, you use three to five colors that are right next to each other on the color wheel. For example, you might choose green, blue-green, blue, and blue-purple. These colors will look good together because they are not very different from each other. Similarly, you can use a color scheme that uses only the *warm colors* (reds, yellows, and oranges), or only the *cool colors* (blues, greens, and purples). The examples in figures 4-11, 4-12, and 4-13 demonstrate analogous design.

The only thing to be cautious of with analogous colors is contrast. They are so similar that they don't provide much contrast, which can be a problem when your text and your background are analogous. To see if they contrast enough, move about five to ten feet away from your monitor, or squint while you are looking at the screen. If the text becomes hard to

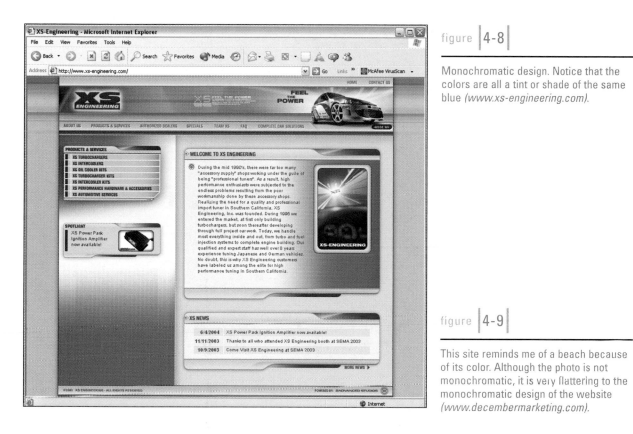

figure |4-8|

Monochromatic design. Notice that the colors are all a tint or shade of the same blue *(www.xs-engineering.com)*.

figure |4-9|

This site reminds me of a beach because of its color. Although the photo is not monochromatic, it is very flattering to the monochromatic design of the website *(www.decembermarketing.com)*.

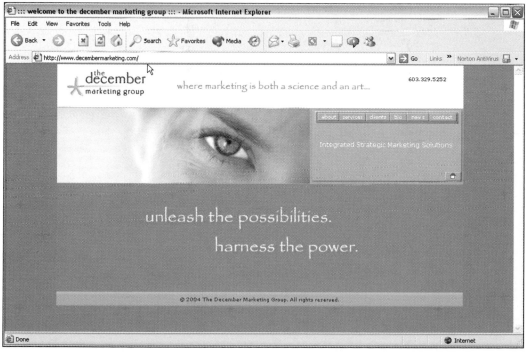

figure | 4-10 |

This site looks very modern as a result of the small digital type and the mint green monochromatic design *(www.papeldigital.pt)*.

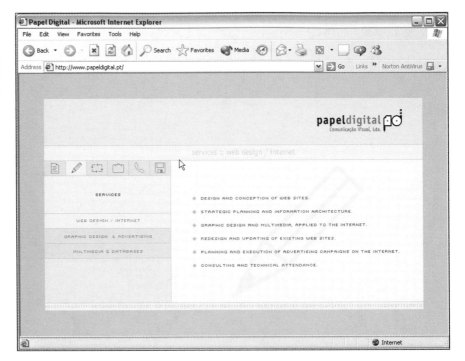

figure | 4-11 |

Analogous colors usually look great together, because they are so similar *(www.fahrenheit.com/main.html)*.

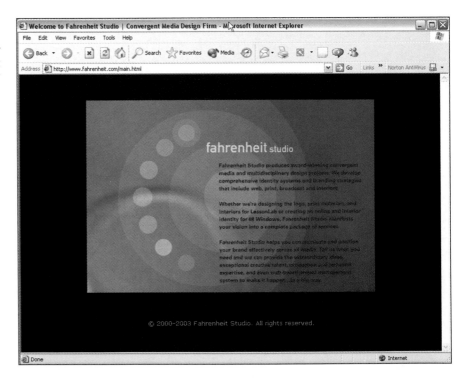

figure 4-12

On this site, you can see clearly that the colors range from yellow to dark red. The analogous colors are all in the warm palette *(www.itcatmedia.com/school).*

figure 4-13

This sports site shows the range of analogous colors, moving from blue to green to yellow *(www.pulseworks.tv/index3.htm).*

see and blends into the background, there's not enough contrast. You can fix this problem without changing your color scheme by using a tint or a shade that is drastically lighter or darker than the surrounding colors (figure 4-14).

figure |4-14|

Can you read the text in the top image? Reading text on a website shouldn't be this difficult! The bottom image uses more contrast, making it much easier to read.

Complementary

The **complementary** color scheme simply uses colors that are opposite one another on the color wheel. This creates a bold difference between the colors, which makes them stand out. For example, if you put blue and orange together, the orange really stands out against the blue; it stands out so much, in fact, that the colors seem to vibrate where they touch. Try red and green; these are even worse! This vibration can be painful to the eyes, and make it uncomfortable for the viewer (figure 4-15).

figure |4-15|

You can see how painful complementary colors can be to look at when placed together! Notice how the colors seem to vibrate where they touch.

This can be an especially bad combination if your background and text are complementary colors (figure 4-16). So, while the complementary colors can be used to make a bold contrast, they must be used with care. Here's a good tip: if you want to combine the boldness of complementary colors without the painful vibration, try surrounding the overlying color with an outline of some other color or white, as demonstrated in figures 4-17, 4-18, and 4-19. This is much easier to look at!

figure |4-16|

Using complementary colors for the background and text is one of the greatest sins of web design.

It is especially hard to read text when the text color and the background are complements of one another.

figure |4-17|

White takes away the pain of complementary text and background. Now the text is easy to read!

figure |4-18|

Although the complementary colors touch in this image, the use of a darker shade of blue makes the effect less harsh *(www.i360.net/).*

figure |4-19|

Using neutral colors can also help to play down the strong contrast of complementary colors.

Split Complementary

A **split complementary** color scheme takes the power of the complementary colors just left of center. Well actually, left and right of center. To get a split complementary scheme, select your color, and then look to the color wheel for its complement. Then look at the colors that border the complement on each side. For example, if you choose orange as your main color, you won't use it with its complementary blue, but with blue-purple and blue-green (see figures 4-20 and 4-21).

figure 4-20

Split complementary design, with bold results *(www.thecookingguy.com)*.

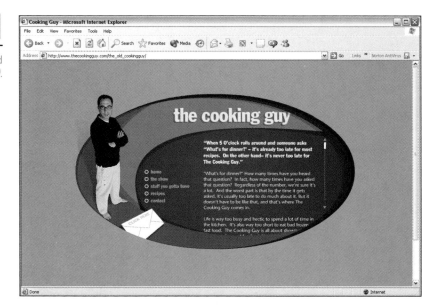

figure 4-21

This split complementary design is more subtle, but is still eye-catching *(www.claudia-stein-design.de)*.

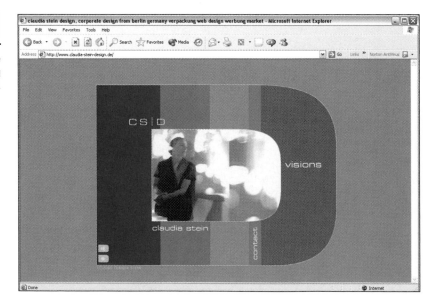

Double Contrast

Double contrast also bases itself in complementary colors, but taking it one step further. You choose your main color and its complement—for example, yellow and purple. Then you choose the colors on the right, next to your main colors. So if your complementary colors are yellow and purple, you would choose blue-purple, red-purple, yellow-green, and yellow-orange as your colors to design with. These combinations can produce some bold and sometimes retro-looking effects (figure 4-22).

figure | 4-22 |

This image shows how vivid and bright a double contrast can be.

Triadic

Triadic is based on three colors that are equal distances apart on the color wheel. If you draw lines to connect the three colors, it will form a triangle. For example, the three primary colors—red, yellow, and blue—form a triadic color scheme. Triadic colors go well together, yet still distinctly contrast (figures 4-23 and 4-24).

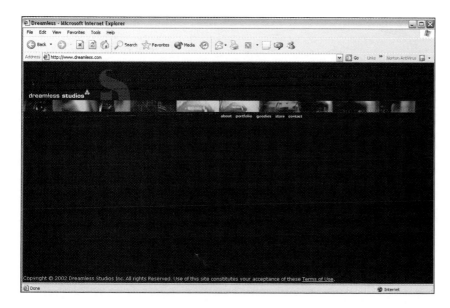

figure | 4-23 |

Triadic designs are often used for children's sites. However, this figure shows that they can also be used to create a mature design (www.dreamless.com).

figure | 4-24 |

Triadic design is great
for attracting attention
(www.ezitsolutions.com/
main/index.php).

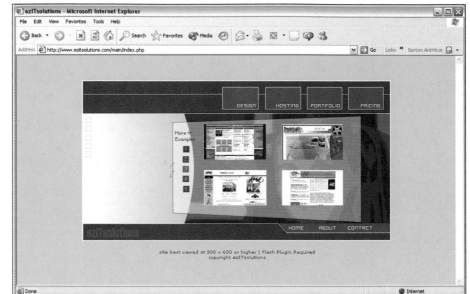

You don't have to stick to these color combinations alone; they are just some good suggestions. There are plenty of others, which you can observe by surfing the Web and looking at other websites. And of course, you can always create your own!

WHITE AND BLACK

Color schemes give you a starting place, but they don't solve all your problems for you. If there is text on the site (and there usually will be), it's not a great idea to use colored text on a colored background. It's simply not that easy to read. However, there is a solution: use white and black!

White and black are generally not considered actual colors. As we mentioned earlier, they are values of colors. This sort of takes them right out of the color wheel. However, since they don't really fit in the wheel, it frees you to use them with any color.

In design, you will hear people refer to **white space**. This is literally the white space on your website. Most designers use white space to provide distance between colors that might not work well right next to each other. Using a lot of white space on your site can give it a fresh, clean appearance. Using white space between your colors can make each color seem more bold, and can sometimes illustrate the differences better than putting the colors right against each other. And of course, it's much easier to read text that's on the white space. On white space, you can even get away with colored text, as long as it's not a very light tint (figure 4-25).

Some designers will use black in place of white space. Black websites are bold, and very appealing, especially to younger users. Colors look different on black and white backgrounds (figure 4-26), and frankly, almost everything looks really cool on a black background. But black may simply be too cool for most sites! Sure, it's great if you're creating a website for a new action film, but it may just be a little too cool for a bank. When using black, remember your audience; do they want a bank that is hip, cool, and elite? Probably not, and I'll bet the bank would prefer not to project an image of being too cool for their customers, either.

Finally, when using black, remember that it's not easy to read a lot of text on a black background, even if the text is white. If the site contains a lot of writing, it's best not to use a black background; or if you must use black, then provide a little white space for the reading.

figure | 4-25 |

Compare these sites. The second is much easier to read because of the white space, and the borders of the shapes lined in white are also more distinct.

figure | 4-26 |

Here, you can see the difference in the appearance of the colors against the black and white backgrounds.

PACK YOUR BRAIN

rose gonnella

Rose Gonnella is an educator, artist, designer, and writer. Rose has exhibited her art nationally and internationally in collections such as Smithsonian National Museum of American Art. She has also authored numerous books and articles on creativity, art, and architecture.

Why are some professional artists and designers or students of the arts bubbling fonts of creativity that flow with a seemingly endless stream of ideas? Energetically creative people weren't born with minds filled with visual and mental information. Ideas spring from a brain (and heart) packed with experience and knowledge. Creative people are curious and passionate about learning. Curiosity is the foundation of creativity. Creative people fuel their brains everyday by absorbing as much mental and visual stimuli as can be tolerated before passing out at the end of an evening. Even in sleep, creative people find ideas. Upon waking, a creative person will jot down the weird and wacky juxtapositions of imagery and dialogue that come during a dream.

Inspiration and ideas are products of proactive minds. Creative people are listeners, doers, hobbyists, collectors, museum-goers, travelers, scavengers, revelers, searchers, adventurers—with the exploring done through far-reaching experience or simply by reading books. Creative people are hunters and gatherers who constantly look and fill their living space with interesting scraps of paper, all sorts of printed matter, oddly-shaped paper clips, do-dads, gadgets, and, of course, books. Creative people take notes, yet understand that what they accumulate on any given day probably has no particular immediate purpose. Creative people invest in learning and searching for its own sake. The search for inspiration and ideas is an investment. Time is needed to sponge up information from a myriad of sources. Time is needed to experience. And, in time, your brain fills up with all manner of stimulation. The stored information, images, and ideas are calmly waiting to be reordered, reconfigured, refreshed, and put to creative use. The stockpile lies dormant until a spark ignites it: you are asked to find a solution to a creative problem. And BANG!—stored information explodes and ideas pop.

But you can't pull out of your head what is not in your head. Creativity does not happen in a vacuum. You have to pack your brain (fortunately there is always room for more). When you ask the question "how do I get a great idea?" the response is: reach into your brain and yank it out, OR get up, get out, and gather what you need. Research. Excellent ideas come from what pre-exists in your brain from previous research, discovery, and exploration or from what you actively put there for the instance. If you are designing a brochure to "save the whales," it is time that you a.) went on a whale watch, b.) watched a documentary about whales, c.) visited a public aquarium that has whales, or d.) read and searched the Web. But don't rely on the Web alone. Experience comes best with personal field experiences.

WHAT DO TEETH HAVE TO DO WITH TEA BAGS? Nothing. Isolated visual and intellectual information gathered for the pure joy and pleasure of savaging, searching, research, observation, or accidental discovery (such as visiting a flea market, reading a book on Northwest Coast Indian masks, poking through the Japanese bookstore near Rockefeller Center in New York City, bird watching, or coming upon a mural by Thomas Hart Benton at the city hall in Jefferson City, Missouri) will not be useful until the material is compared, related, combined, synthesized, and composed. Meaning comes from relationships. Keeping your mind wide open to comparing and combining disparate objects, ideas, and imagery creates visual poetry and fresh ideas. A design found on the ceiling of the Uffizi Gallery in Florence might make a great composition juxtaposed with an image of clouds. In isolation, an image of clouds is seen as itself. Seen together, an image of a floral tapestry and clouds may suggest an entirely new and evocative meaning. Some people look into the night sky and see stars. Creative people look at the stars and also see horses, crabs, lions, and warriors. Now, what do teeth have to do with tea bags? Open your mind and let the possibilities pour in.

WEB-SAFE COLOR IS ALMOST DEAD!

Hexadecimal is a system of numbers and letters used to translate colors into a code that your computer can understand. With hexadecimal you can set colors for the text, links, and background on your websites. It is the color system for the Web, and is used because your computer may not understand what specific color you want when you enter "red," but it will understand FF0000. Not only will it understand that, but it will also know the difference between that red and 990000, 330000, CC6666, and even 8D1509! All of these hexadecimal codes will give you red, but they are all different values of red. Hexadecimal tells your computer which value to use.

When talking about hexadecimal, you'll inevitably come across the **web-safe color palette** (this, by the way, is called by a few different names, but if you come across something with the words "color," "safe," "216," or "palette" in the name, and it seems to exist just to limit your choices for web colors, it's probably the same thing). The web-safe color palette is a set of 216 colors that can be viewed on almost any color monitor, regardless of the video card it has. The web-safe palette was created for 8-bit (or 256 color) computer systems. Nowadays, most computers are able to show far more than 256 colors. So you can pretty much call the web-safe color palette dead. If that seems harsh, consider that the web-safe color palette not only uses just 216 colors, but they aren't even very good colors to begin with (figure 4-27). Most of them are oversaturated and clash with one another, and there are not enough soft, muted tones. Say, for example, that you are designing a site for a store's autumn line of clothing. You decide to use a vanilla cream and a soft, suede brown to reflect the colors of the clothes. You go to the web-safe color palette and find that these colors don't exist there! Using the 216-color palette, you find you are stuck with a too-bright lemon yellow and a too-warm brown the color of melted chocolate (figure 4-28). You've gone from elegant to obnoxious in one easy step!

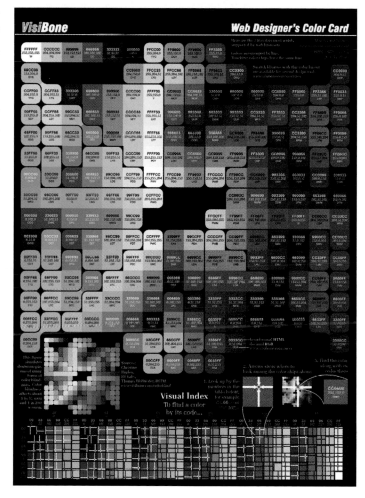

figure | 4-27 |

The web-safe color palette, although usually too limiting for practical use, must be used at times. We recommend VisiBone's comprehensive resources when you need to find the right color (www.visibone.com).

figure |4-28|

The first image represents how we want our fall line to look: cool and classy. The second image is in web-safe colors, and reminds us a bit too much of melted chocolate on a sunny day.

For this very reason, most designers do not use the web-safe color palette anymore to design websites. The fact that there are only 216 unappealing colors to choose from is a big headache for designers, and most computers are modern enough to display the colors properly. Even if they don't, most designers would rather take the chance of the color not displaying properly than accept a limit of 216 colors. Keep in mind that all colors will look slightly different on another monitor, even if the colors are web safe, because monitor settings will differ between all computers. Just to make sure that you are designing for the masses, it's a good idea to go out and check your website on other computers. Public library computers are especially good; they are free to use in most places, and are usually not top of the line machines, so you will get a good real-world feel for your site!

There is one situation in which the web-safe color palette is still used. If you are making a website for a client who has a logo or signature product colors that must always appear in the same color, it is a good idea to use the web-safe color palette. You will need to match the client's color preferences to the nearest match on the web-safe color palette. Once this is done, you can ensure that this color will be very close to the same on most computers.

CONSIDER THE COLOR BLIND

Did you know that one in twelve people has a color deficiency? Considering those numbers, it's important to make sure that these people can see your website as easily as anyone else. In Chapter 5, page 111, color blindness is discussed in great detail. The main thing is to maintain contrast, which is especially important with text. Make sure the text has enough contrast to look different to people who are color blind. Frankly, those who are not color blind will also thank you; those colors that aren't easy for the color blind to see are usually not easy for the rest of the world to read. To make sure you have enough contrast in your image or between your text and your background, try this: convert the whole thing to **grayscale** (which is just a fancy term for black and white). If you can't tell the colors apart easily in gray, they may be difficult for a color blind person to see (figure 4-29). Even for people who are not color blind, there may not be enough contrast for important site elements to be distinct.

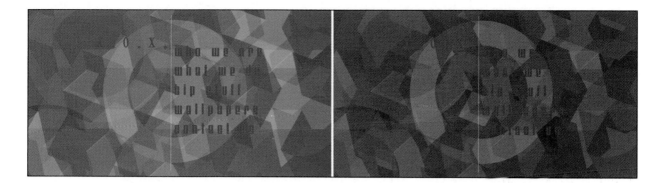

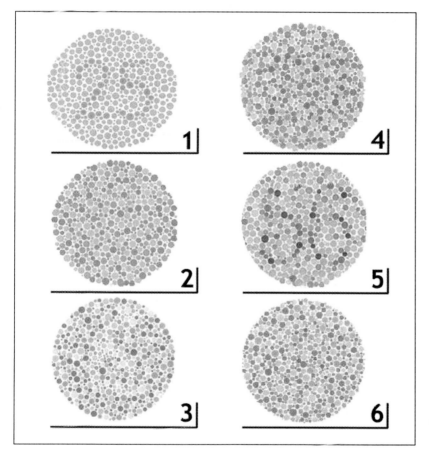

figure |4-29|

The text in this image may be almost impossible for color blind persons to distinguish. Notice how the lack of contrast is emphasized in the grayscale version.

figure |4-30|

Many people with red-green color blindness don't even realize they have it. We all just assume that everyone sees colors the same way we do. Here is a test you can use to determine whether you're color blind. The table below explains what you should see.

Figure 5-20 on page 112 is this figure in grayscale. Note that the grayscale version lacks enough contrast for even noncolor-blind viewers to see the numbers.

table |4-1|

Red-green color blindness test results.

Normal Color Vision			Red-Green Color Blind		
	Left	Right		Left	Right
Top (1 and 4)	25	29	Top (1 and 4)	25	Spots
Middle (2 and 5)	45	56	Middle (2 and 5)	Spots	56
Bottom (3 and 6)	6	8	Bottom (3 and 6)	Spots	Spots

THE WEB DESIGN ARTIST AT WORK

Jonas Strandberg-Ringh

Job Title: Graphic designer

Organization: Freelance

Number of years in field: Six

Partial client list: DigitalVision, Uni Lever, VH1

Websites: http://www.cubadust.com

What type of work do you do?

I try to keep a healthy balance between web, print, and motion design, but of course, there are periods when I tend to lean in one direction.

The web projects I take on are usually for midsized companies or start-up businesses. What I love about working with new companies is that it's fun knowing that I will help give them their "personality." It's too much work for one person to handle a full-blown site for a large company. When I am involved with larger web projects, I focus mainly on the layout and I outsource the backend work.

What got you interested in this field?

I've been a creative person for as long as I can remember, although I can't really say that I knew I would be a graphic designer. I don't have a formal design education; instead, I went to fine art schools and spent most of my younger days painting on canvas and taking photo classes. Then one day I got my first computer and a copy of Photoshop, and I got hooked. It has been my passion ever since.

How do you find your clients?

To be honest I don't find clients, they tend to find me. I made a name for myself as one of the foremost designers during the 3D abstract trend in 1998-99. My site (www.cubadust.com) became widely known in the online design community. The name of my site still gets spread around by word of mouth and noticed by companies across the globe who then contact me for freelance work. I am mostly known as a web/print designer though, so I have often put together motion reels to promote this other part of my business.

How do you decide what to charge for your services?

I have a set hourly rate, but it may vary depending on the nature of the project.

What type of hardware/software do you use?

I use a Pentium 4 with a 2GHz processor and 512 MB RAM. It has served me well, but it is starting to show its age, so I will upgrade my system soon.

I use industry standard applications: Photoshop, After Effects, 3D Studio Max, Dreamweaver, and a Canon IXUS 500 digital camera.

Where do you find creative inspiration?

There are designers and artists I appreciate more than others, but for my creations I seek inspiration elsewhere. Like everyone else, I get inspired by everything and nothing: interacting with people, reading books and magazines, watch-

DigitalVision image constructed using thirteen separable Photoshop layers. The layers can be mixed, adjusted, enhanced, combined and deconstructed. ©Digital Vision.

How do you think your field will develop in the future, and how do you plan to adapt?

I think the web industry will keep growing stronger and stronger. Today the only things that can stop the depth of content on a site are the designer's and programmer's imaginations. You don't have to worry about people having slow Internet connections in the same way you had to just a few years ago. You've got software developers working around the clock producing applications with only one purpose: web solutions. And of course, all these kids who love this profession have almost made it a lifestyle.

Right now, sites tend to be information-driven. I think this will peak in 2005. With the increased availability of broadband, we will be able to design more heavy loading sites. Let's just hope that designers use it the right way. I really don't want to see sites with ridiculously overworked Flash interfaces just for the sake of it. And I don't want to see sites that use certain techniques just because they're available as a solution, if it's not a good solution.

ing TV, even playing video games. Architecture, nature, and of course, the work itself can be very inspiring. I would like some kind of secret inspiration recipe though, because a bad case of "designer's block" can be awful. I guess it's something that everyone involved with creative work encounters from time to time.

What advice would you give to students interested in pursuing a career in your field?

Never give up. Spend as much time as possible working on new images, layouts, and playing around in Photoshop. Every second you sit in front of your computer and try to produce, you evolve: you learn to get from point A to point B in different ways. Soon you feel more confident and try new things, new techniques, and new styles. It's a never-ending process.

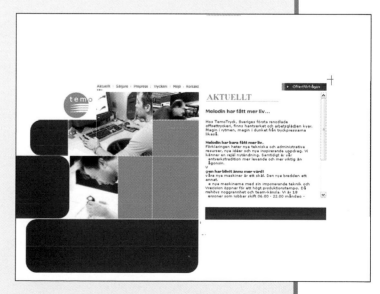

Website design for Temo. ©Temo

figure |4-31|

At times you will want to use red and black, as they make a strong impact. In this example from Chapter 3, white was added around the text to make it more readable for the color blind. See figure 3-8 for a grayscale version of this figure.

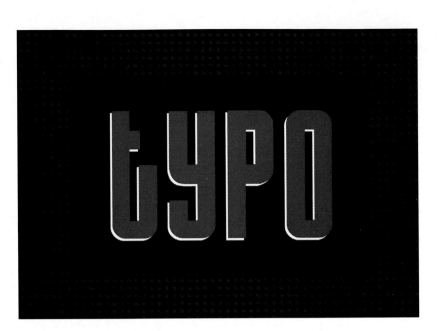

PSYCHOLOGY OF COLOR

Did you know that orange and red make most people hungry while blue is an appetite suppressant? Did you know that green makes many people think of money, health, and tranquility? Colors mean different things to different people, and you can change the effect of your website by understanding how color will affect the viewers. It's important to remember that different cultures have different interpretations of colors. For example, in America we associate pink with girls and blue with boys. However, in China blue is for young girls and black is for young boys. If you plan to use color psychology on your website, know what culture your audience is from, and use colors that have the right meaning for that audience. An in-depth discussion of this topic is beyond the scope of this book; however, many books on this subject do exist, so check your local library or bookstore. You can also find plenty of useful information on the Web.

CHAPTER SUMMARY

Now that you understand the basics of color theory, you should be equipped to use color without abusing it. Be warned that it's much easier to learn the theories than it is to apply them, because it's very easy to get carried away with colors. For now just practice, seek critiques, and practice some more.

in review

1. What is the color wheel?

2. Name the primary colors.

3. Name the secondary colors.

4. Name the intermediate colors.

5. What is color value?

6. Define tint.

7. Define shade.

8. Describe three color schemes.

9. Define monochromatic.

10. Give an example of complementary colors.

11. Give an example of analogous colors. Describe the problem usually encountered with analogous colors.

12. Give an example of warm colors.

13. Give an example of cool colors.

14. What is color psychology? Give examples of meanings attached to three colors in American culture.

exercises

1. Design websites using only colors and shapes (no text, no photos, no illustrations), based on the following themes. For each site, do your best to convey the moods and attitudes associated with that theme. Show your completed design to at least one other person. Ask them what they feel the colors represent, and compare their responses to your goals.
   a. Site: Corporate
   Demographic: wide range of ages and backgrounds
   Desired mood or theme: security, honesty, professionalism
   b. Site: Child-related
   Demographic: children under twelve and parents
   Desired mood or theme: fun, stimulating, impulsive
   c. Site: Extreme Pop Culture
   Demographic: teenage to young adult, mostly male
   Desired mood or theme: exciting, cutting edge, intense

2. Design a website based on a monochromatic color scheme. You must use the same color throughout your design, but you can vary the tint, shade, and saturation as much as you want. You may also include black and white.

3. Choose three of the color schemes we discussed and design one website for each scheme.

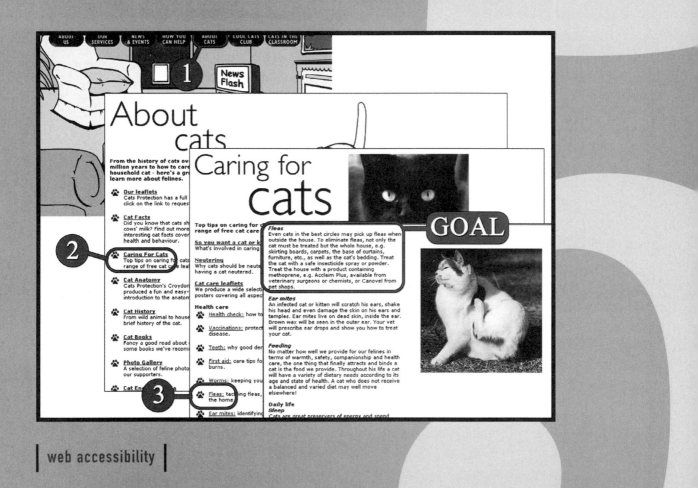

objectives

Understand the meaning and importance of accessibility

Learn some general rules of thumb that make a site usable for everyone

Discover the many different ways people access the Internet

Build a new toolset of design techniques to increase accessibility

introduction

Web accessibility, or usability, simply means *how easy it is to use your web page.* If using your web page is as easy as using a telephone, then you've done pretty well. On the other hand, if people have an easier time programming their VCRs than finding what they want on your web page, you probably need some help in this area.

In order to successfully design a truly accessible website, you have to first understand a few basic things that make your site more successful overall and easier to navigate for everyone. Then you need to break down "everyone" into smaller categories and understand the specific needs of each one. This is important for a variety of reasons. One is to attract as many interested people as possible to your website. Another, more important reason is that it is always good business to be polite, respectful, and considerate of individuals. Remember, the customer is always right. And last but not least, it's the law.

Easy as 1, 2, 3.

figure |5-1|

User-friendly interface.

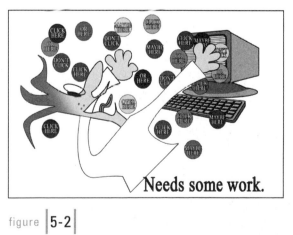

Needs some work.

figure |5-2|

Interface out of control. Unorganized navigation with too many links can overwhelm the user.

THE AMERICANS WITH DISABILITIES ACT

In 1990, Congress passed into law the Americans with Disabilities Act (ADA). It basically states that no one with a disability can be discriminated against by the government or a private company. You can read the specifics yourself at the ADA homepage (figure 5-3). As you may be aware, government agencies and private companies must make reasonable accommodations for the disabled. Even if you aren't aware, I'm sure you've noticed the prevalence in our society of handicapped parking spaces, wheelchair-accessible entrance ramps and restroom stalls, Braille lettering on signs, etc. If you yourself aren't disabled, or don't know someone who is, it can be easy to overlook the necessity of such things. However, a responsible businessperson or civil servant must always strive to make his or her product or service equally available to everyone. The Americans with Disabilities Act stands as a constant reminder of this fact.

So, how does this apply to you as a web designer? In 1996, the Department of Justice formally stated that the ADA also applies to the World Wide Web. Much the same way as a hospital, a post office, or a grocery store needs a wheelchair ramp, websites also need to make certain accommodations to provide easy access to everyone. You may have no idea what I'm talking about at this point, and that's understandable. You can easily visualize a person in a wheelchair using a ramp to gain access to a building, but you may not be able to understand how a blind person could access a web page. Don't fret. That's what this chapter is all about. By the time you're finished, you'll have a good understanding of how different groups of people navigate the Web, and how to make their visit to your site smooth and productive.

THE BIG QUESTIONS

Now that you understand what was meant by breaking "everyone" into smaller categories, let's back up and cover some general rules and concepts that apply all the way across the board. Once we have that basic foundation in place, we'll start building a more detailed understanding on top of it. In this, we're going to go back to the basics. For this section,

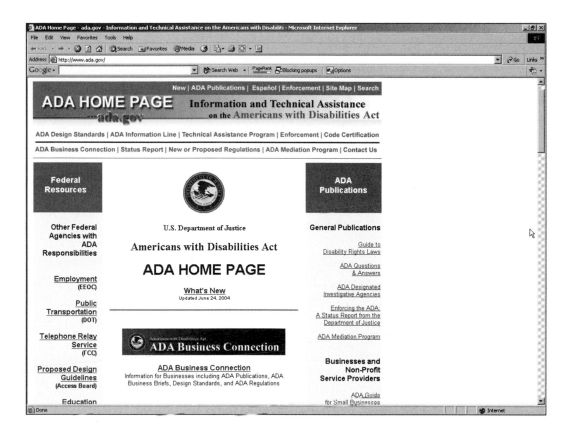

don't just think like a web designer, think of yourself as a web user also. As a web user, there are certain sites you use often, and certain sites you avoid. You don't normally think about it, you just do it. We're going to take a minute to ask ourselves some of the big questions that web users normally answer only by clicking.

figure | 5-3 |

Visit the ADA homepage at *www.usdoj.gov/crt/ada/adahom1.htm.*

Content: Why Am I Here?

Why am I here? Possibly the biggest question of them all, and definitely beyond the scope of this book. We can narrow it down a bit, though. Why am I here, at this particular website? That's better. Let's say you're a cat enthusiast. You're looking for a website about cats. You type *cats* into a search engine, click on a link, and you're off. Once that first page loads, how long do you think you'll stay before you find some information about cats that appeals to you? Twenty seconds? Ten seconds? Remember, your search engine returned three million links to websites about cats. That search page is just one click away.

As a web designer, your job is to make people visit, stay, and revisit your website. How do you do that? Simple. You give them what they want. Don't engage in false advertising. If your website claims to be the end-all authority on cats, make sure you can deliver (figures 5-4 and 5-5). If the research that goes into the content of the site is part of your job description, make sure you do it well. Do your best to present the content in a straightforward and logical order. Make it a point to know what things are most frequently viewed and requested by users, and with that knowledge, give the most popular and interesting information a prominent place in your site. Keep in mind that this information must be interesting to the user.

figure | 5-4 |

You can see this kind of amateur site all over the Web. It's fine for a personal hobby site, but how many people in the world would really be interested in spending time reading about Poodles and Geezer?

Welcome to my cat page

These are my cats, Poodles (left) and Geezer (right). They are both from the same litter and are about 4 months old. Geezer got his name because he has white hair growing out of his ears like an old man. Poodles does too, but he just looked like a "Poodles". Don't you think so? This picture is very indicative of their personalities. Geezer is very curious and usually seems thoughtful, but too skiddish to actually investigate anything. Poodles, on the other hand, is into *everything*. He sniffs and sniffs and paws and lunges and attacks. Actually, I suppose they complement each other well.

Navigation: Where Am I Going?

Where am I going? Don't you know? Of course you do. By the time you find a website, you usually have something specific in mind that you want. You've done the search engine thing. You probably spent several minutes trying different search terms and whittling down your search results until you have a screen full of promising links. You picked the best one, clicked it, and that's where you are. What now? Can you tell immediately from the

figure | 5-5 |

The Cats Protection website *(www.cats.org.uk),* the U.K.'s oldest and largest feline welfare charity, offers real content that many cat owners are genuinely interested in.

interface where you should click to find the thing you're looking for? How long do you think you'll look before backing up and choosing another site? Probably not very long. This is why it's so important to have user-friendly navigation. **Navigation** refers to the way our menu links are structured. It's the way you travel from one page to the next, and back again. Unlike Hansel and Gretel, the user doesn't have a fistful of bread crumbs, so it's up to the designer to make sure no one gets lost.

Grandmothers, Cats, and Clear Navigation

My grandmother is over ninety years old. She thinks computers will be the downfall of society. She has never touched a computer. In fact, she probably hasn't even seen one up close. Any mention of them is usually followed by a disapproving look, shaking of the head, and a lecture. Because of this, she is the perfect instrument with which to hypothetically test the success of my navigation. As I am laying out the navigation for my website, I ask myself, "If someone asked my grandmother to navigate this website, could she do it?" Think of the most computer-illiterate person you know. If that person was asked to navigate your site—assuming they know how to use a mouse—is the navigation clear enough for them to figure it out? If the answer is no, then you need to make some changes.

Let's go back to the cat website example. You may think it's cute to use nameless icons in the navigation bar (a food dish, a rubber mouse, a collar, a pet bed). You may think it's perfectly obvious that the pet bed is the link to the homepage, and the rubber mouse is the link to recreational tips for cat lovers. Trust me, it isn't. Creative expression must never get in the way of practicality. Even if someone thinks your site is cute, they aren't going to stay there very long if they can't find what they're looking for. Make sure your navigation is obvious. Clearly mark every link on your site with labels that accurately describe the content to which they lead.

figure |5-6|

Every once in a while you'll encounter a site where, for artistic reasons, the links are not labeled. Most people find it annoying rather than fun to guess where they go.

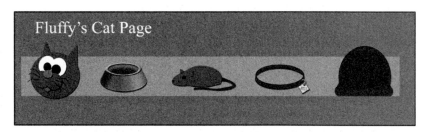

figure |5-7|

Cats Protection *(www.cats.org.uk)*, the U.K.'s largest cat protection website, offers clearly marked links that are very descriptive of the content to which they lead.

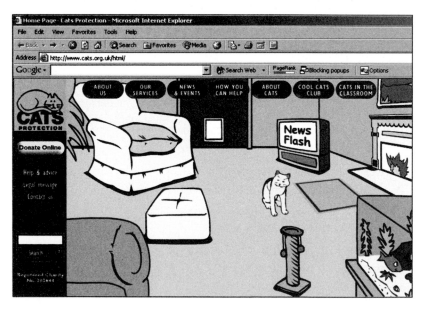

Not only do you need to have your links clearly labeled, but you also need to have a menu that is set apart from the rest of the content. People in a hurry (who isn't in a hurry these days?) aren't interested in sifting through pages of text, hoping to find what they're looking for. When you arrive at a site looking for a specific article, you probably want to read the whole article, but *only* that article. Do you really want to read a homepage full of text describing who made the site and why they put it together? How about a page of text explaining where the various articles are culled from, how many people have found them helpful, and comments from previous visitors? If you enjoy wasting time sifting through irrelevant material, you are most certainly in the minority. What I'm saying is that information on a website should always be *scannable*—you should always be able to read it at a glance. Any extra details should be available on a separate linked page. Compare the two examples in figures 5-8 and 5-9 and see which one you find more appealing.

Geezer's Articles

The articles listed on this page were taken with permission from several different magazines: <u>SuperCat</u>, <u>CatWorld</u>, <u>MeowMeow</u>, <u>Forever Feline</u>, <u>Everything Cat</u>. The editors of these magazines believe that if we give you a taste of the type of articles they publish, you might want to try them for yourself. I highly recommend that you do. For information on subscribing to any one of these, <u>click here</u>.

Many visitors to this website have found exactly what they were looking for in one of the featured articles. Mary from Albertsville writes, "My cat just wouldn't eat her food anymore, but the article from CatWorld about <u>dietary supplements</u> did the trick." David from Cleveland says, "If not for that article on <u>giving CPR to animals</u>, my cat would have died. Thanks from both of us, SuperCat!" Send us your <u>comments here</u>.

The articles are divided into several categories: <u>Accessories</u> deals with everything from kitty-claw-clippers to cat-sweaters. If you have questions about what to feed your cat, or why their eating habits change, you might find some help in <u>Diet</u>. <u>Grooming</u> deals with brushing, bathing, trimming, and dental issues. <u>Health</u> speaks for itself. How long will your cat live, and what can you do to ensure as long a life as possible? Answer these questions in our <u>Longevity</u> section. Dispel some ancient myths about cats and learn some historical facts in our <u>Myths</u> section. <u>Stories</u> are interesting anecdotes shared by visitors to our site. Anything else will fall under the category of <u>General Care</u>. We hope you find what you're looking for. Happy hunting!

figure **5-8**

Sites that bury their links inside a page of text can be frustrating, to say the least.

Geezer's Articles

ARITCLES FROM VARIOUS MAGAZINES
(sources listed within each article)

SUBJECTS COVERED:
<u>Accessories</u>
<u>Diet</u>
<u>General Care</u>
<u>Grooming</u>
<u>Health</u>
<u>Longevity</u>
<u>Myths</u>
<u>Stories</u>

Click <u>here</u> for testimonials and suggestions from readers.

Click <u>here</u> for information on subscribing to one or more of these magazines.

figure **5-9**

Although still not pretty, this page is much better organized and can be navigated quickly and efficiently.

The Three-Click Rule

If your website has a lot of pages, it will be nearly impossible to provide a link to every one of them on your homepage. Even if you could, users would become frustrated trying to sort through them all. For that reason, you need to group similar sets of links together and organize them in categories from general to specific. In the case of our cat website, let's say you're looking for an article about ridding your cat of fleas. You could click a menu link called "Articles." That would lead to a new menu that contains different subjects of articles (behavior, grooming, health, accessories, etc.). From this menu, you would click "Health" and be shown a new menu, listing the titles of articles about cat health care. So you see how the menu was set up logically from general to specific (Articles > Health > *How Do I Fight Feline Fleas?*). The main thing to notice here is that you were able to reach the correct article without clicking more than three times. A good rule of thumb is to make everything on your website reachable within three clicks. Why three clicks? Think about how many clicks you're willing to make before you get frustrated and go somewhere else. It depends on your level of patience and how much of a hurry you're in, but for the average person there's no reason to bother beyond three. Not when there are thousands or millions of other sites out there containing similar information.

figure | 5-10 |

Once again, the Cats Protection website *(www.cats.org.uk)*, the U.K.'s largest cat protection website, provides our example. Notice that you can reach the article about fleas in just three clicks.

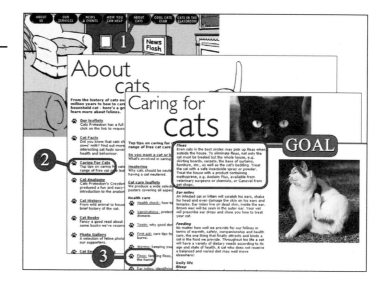

Summary of the Basics

Everything we've just discussed comes down to this: keep it simple. Simple is elegant, clean, memorable, user-friendly. Keeping the content simple means giving the users what they want. If you have more than they want, that's great. Don't force it on them. Put it in a separate and clearly marked location. If someone wants it, they'll know where to find it. Keeping the navigation simple means having a menu that is easy to read and easy to understand. Keep the structure of your site organized and logical, with every page no more than three clicks from any other. Master these concepts, and you'll be ahead of the game.

DISABILITIES AND THE WEB

It is estimated that in most populations, ten to twenty percent of the people are disabled. The President's Committee on Employment of People with Disabilities found that the United States is at the high end of this statistic, with nearly one in five Americans considered disabled in some way. Not every disability affects a person's ability to effectively navigate the Web, but many do. These range from minor inconveniences to debilitating conditions. If you work for a company with at least fifteen employees, you are required by law to make reasonable accommodations for people with disabilities. In this section, we'll explain how to do that on your website.

The W3C and the Web Accessibility Initiative

The World Wide Web Consortium (or W3C) is an organization that was formed in 1994 and has about five hundred member organizations from all over the world. The director is none other than Tim Berners-Lee, the man who invented the World Wide Web. The W3C is responsible for standardizing the code of the Web. Imagine if every electrical outlet in your house had a different kind of interface. Your toaster might plug into the outlet in the living room, but not in the kitchen. Your alarm clock might plug into the outlet in the bathroom, but not in the bedroom. What a mess that would be. We don't have those problems because when the whole "electrical outlet" thing for the Web got started, someone said, "Hey, wouldn't this be easier if we made it all work the same way?" That's what the W3C is doing with the Web. Due to the standards they create, you can access a website in Australia just as easily as one in Texas. If you'd like more information about the W3C, or want to take a look at the standards they set, you can visit their website at *www.w3c.org.*

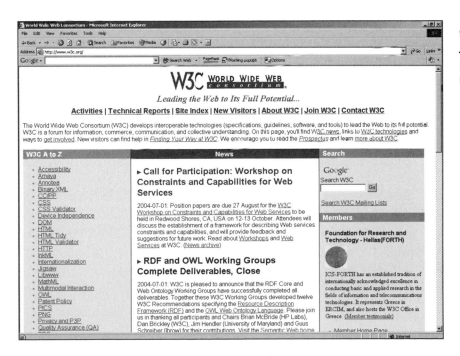

figure |5-11|

Homepage of the World Wide Web Consortium *(www.w3c.org).*

figure | 5-12 |

Homepage of the World Wide Web
Consortium's Web Accessibility Initiative
(www.w3c.org/wai).

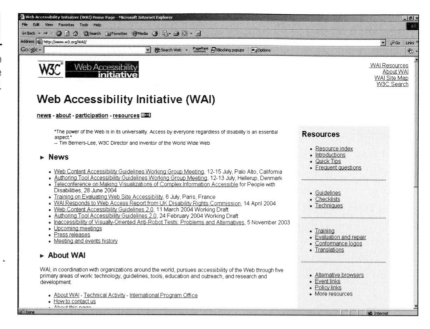

figure | 5-13 |

Homepage of the World Wide Web
Consortium's Web Accessibility Initiative;
the W3C Accessibility Checklist
(www.w3c.org/TR/WCAG10/).

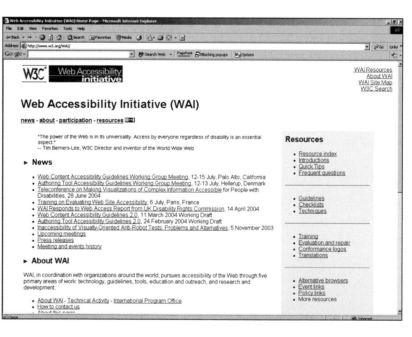

The Web Accessibility Initiative is a branch of the W3C that is concerned
with, you guessed it, accessibility. Check out their site at *www.w3c.org/WAI.*
Here you can find up-to-date information about all aspects of disabilities
that relate to the Web, including laws and legal precedents in many
countries around the world. They have even put together an accessibility
checklist to help keep you organized *(www.w3c.org/TR/WCAG10/).* This
checklist is divided into three categories: Priority 1: things you must fix;

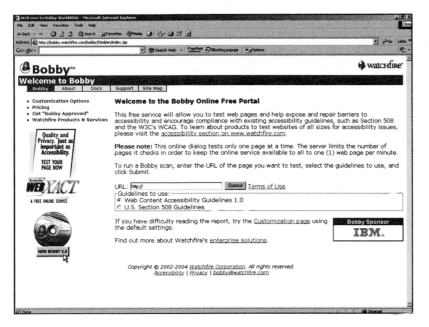

figure |5-14|

Test your accessibility with Bobby
(www.cast.org/bobby), provided
by the Watchfire Corporation
(www.watchfire.com).

Priority 2: things you *should* fix; and Priority 3: things you may fix to make sure the greatest number of people has access to your site. There is another site called Bobby *(www.cast.org/bobby/)* that will check every aspect of your website for free and evaluate it according to the WAI accessibility standards. Don't overtax it, though. It's a free service, and you're only allowed one scan per minute.

Blindness

According to the U.S. Census, nearly two million Americans are legally blind, and almost eight million have serious visual impairments. The World Wide Web is a visual medium, so how can a person who can't see well (or see at all) access your site? There have been marvelous advances in technology, such as text-to-speech translators (devices that read the text on your page out loud) and Braille translators (devices that convert text into raised dots on a Teflon display panel).

So with all these translators available, what's the problem? One problem is that the translators are not intelligent. They can only read text that's there on the page. They can't add anything to it. For example, if you have images on your website, the translator program can't examine the pictures and describe them. When it scans space containing an image, if there's nothing there but that image, it draws a blank. You can imagine that if there are many such images on your page, a visually impaired user will be missing

figure |5-15|

The BrailleNote PK is the world's smallest
blindness personal digital assistant.
Image provided by Pulse Data
Humanware *(www.pulsedata.com).*

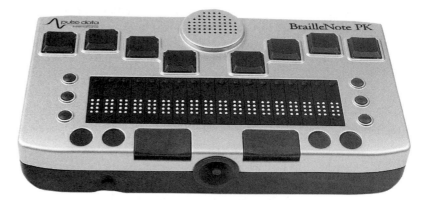

figure |5-16|

The BrailleNote QT 32 features speech
output, a refreshable Braille display, and
a computer-style keyboard. Image
provided by Pulse Data Humanware
(www.pulsedata.com).

figure |5-17|

The VoiceNote QT speech output
keyboard. Image provided by Pulse Data
Humanware *(www.pulsedata.com).*

most of what you have to offer. So what can you do about this? Inside the structure of your web page (the HTML code), you can include something called an ALT tag with every image. Have you ever placed your mouse over an image on a web page and seen a little text box pop up with a title for the image (figure 5-18)? That's what an ALT tag does. It supplies brief descriptive text with an image. A translator program can pick this up, and use it to describe the image, as long as the ALT tag is descriptive and not something like "pic-1." One more helpful thing you can do is if an image is also a hyperlink, include that in the ALT tag (for example, *LINK: gallery page*).

figure |5-18|

The ALT tag displays a text box that says "LINK: writers click to log in." Notice also that since the WRITERS bubble is a link, the designer identified it as a link with the ALT tag.

Another problem is that translator programs read in a logical order instead of scanning around the page to find what users want; they read left to right and top to bottom. As long as there is a menu at the top of the page, this shouldn't be a problem. Just keep this in mind when you design the layout of your pages. If you feel that you absolutely must express your artistic style by laying out your pages in an unconventional way, then be considerate and include a link to a more conventional version of your site.

Another important consideration is how a visually impaired person will navigate around your page. You're probably used to simply moving your mouse to the appropriate section and clicking. This is called *focusing* the cursor. The problem is, if you can't see the page, how do you know where to focus the cursor? The most common alternative way to navigate is to use the TAB key. The TAB key allows you to move to the next element of a web page that is recognized by a browser as a *tab stop*. Try it the next time you go online. Use TAB to go forward and SHIFT + TAB to go backward. So, how do you create tab stops? *Anchor* tags, the tags you use to create hyperlinks, are always tab stops. So, TAB will automatically take you from hyperlink to hyperlink. Elements within a form (by form, I just mean one of those lists that you fill out online) are also tab stops, as are frames. If your site is organized with tables, you can include *table headers* in your HTML code (by using the TITLE attribute—see the Selected HTML Glossary sidebar, page 116) that identify the content of each section. You can also use the TABINDEX attribute in each table cell tag to turn it into a tab stop. Once the table cell becomes a tab stop, the user can skip through them quickly. This makes navigation much quicker and easier for those who must wait for the text reader to read the content to them. If a user decides that a section is irrelevant, they can move on to the next one immediately.

These are not the only ways you can improve the accessibility of your site, but the main purpose of this section is to familiarize you with the concept of designing for those users with disabilities. Now that you're aware of these issues, a little common sense planning can go a long way. Talk to those you know who have disabilities and ask what problems they encounter when dealing with the Web. You can also find plenty of information online. The best way to begin, as we mentioned earlier, is by consulting the World Wide Web Consortium Web Accessibility Initiative *(www.w3c.org/WAI)*.

Other Visual Disabilities: Low Vision and Color Blindness

First of all, it is important to clarify that low vision and color blindness are not the same thing. They are treated together in this section because the same design solution can be successful in both cases. Both of these affect a significant amount of the population, and should not be overlooked in your design process.

Low Vision

More than eleven million people in the United States suffer from low vision. A person is said to have low vision if clear vision cannot be achieved through the use of corrective lenses. Many of the accessibility solutions for blindness can also help people with low vision, but as they are not blind, there are some additional things a designer can do to meet their particular needs. Low vision means a person can still see, and probably see well enough to perform many tasks, but reading small text characters on a website would not be among them. There are a number of ways to make screen text bigger. For example, there are built-in screen magnifiers that are standard in Windows and Macintosh operating systems, as well as external hardware that magnifies the screen itself. However, text size is not always the problem. Certain fonts make it hard for some people to distinguish characters, as well. A person with low vision may have a particular font that is ideally suited to their particular condition. Wouldn't it be perfect if your users could pick their own font to display text? Actually, they can with a little help from you.

A good solution to this problem is for designers to use **style sheets** when designing their pages. Commonly referred to in web design software as CSS (Cascading Style Sheets), this feature is basically a customizable list of fonts and properties that are automatically assigned to any web page that references it (figure 5-19). The time-saving benefits to designers are enormous, since multiple web pages can be reformatted at once by simply changing the style sheet. The benefit to your users is that they can override your style sheets with style sheets of their own. Most of the major web browsers, including Internet Explorer and Netscape Navigator, will allow a user to apply a personalized style sheet to any web page that accepts them. It's a win-win situation.

figure | 5-19 |

```
 1  /*dog vision styles*/
 2  /*text elements*/
 3
 4  body {
 5      text-align:center;
 6      margin: 0px;
 7      background-color: #666666;
 8      font-family: "MS Sans Serif", Verdana, Arial, sans-serif;
 9      font-size: 10px;
10      color: #000000;
11  }
12
13  a:link, a:visited, a:active {
14      font-family: "MS Sans Serif", Verdana, Arial, sans-serif;
15      color: #000000;
16      font-size: 10px;
17      text-decoration: underline
18  }
19
20  a:hover {
21      font-family: "MS Sans Serif", Verdana, Arial, sans-serif;
22      color: #000000;
23      font-size: 10px;
24      background-color: #E0E0E0;
25  }
26
27  a.hidden:link, a.hidden:visited, a.hidden:active, a.hidden:hover {
28      font-family: "MS Sans Serif", Verdana, Arial, sans-serif;
29      color: #000000;
30      font-size: 10px;
31      text-decoration: none
32  }
33
34  .heavy {
35      font-weight: bold;
36  }
37
38  /*layout elements*/
```

This is an example of a typical CSS (Cascading Style Sheet).

Color Blindness

Color blindness is not really blindness at all. It is also a common misconception that people who are color blind see in black and white. Such a condition does exist, called achromatopsia, but it is very rare, striking only about one person in thirty-three thousand. The most common type of color blindness is **red-green color blindness.** It is almost exclusively confined to males, affecting eight percent of all males and only one-half of one percent of females. The results are not a failure to perceive the colors red and green, but an inability to distinguish between them. Since, as we discussed in Chapter 4, all the colors you see on your computer monitor are made from different combinations of red, green and blue, this can be a significant problem. Certain colors of text and background can seem to blend together and become indistinguishable to a color-blind person in a way that a web designer might not be able to anticipate.

figure |5-20|

Compare this image with the color version on page 91 (figure 4-30). A good test of your color combinations is to convert your artwork to grayscale. Here in grayscale, the lack of contrast makes the numbers barely visible, if at all, even to the noncolor-blind viewer.

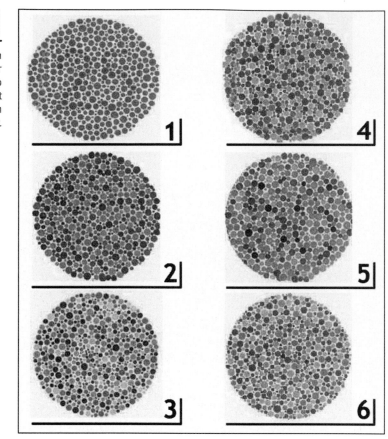

As we mentioned in Chapter 4, a good test to determine how a color-blind person sees your color combinations is to convert your artwork to grayscale. Figure 5-20 is the grayscale version of the color blindness test in figure 4-30 on page 91. Even for a noncolor-blind person, the numbers are barely visible, if at all.

What about those style sheets? You've probably already guessed that they can come in handy here, as well. Not only can style sheets specify fonts, but they can also change the color of text and the background, even turning off patterns or images. Quick application of a personalized style sheet can make that hard-to-read website crystal clear.

Deafness and Hardness of Hearing

The World Wide Web has always been primarily a visual medium. However, now that broadband connections are becoming more prevalent, many sites are experimenting with video and audio content. It is in these areas that people with hearing impairments can have trouble. Any audio file that is presented as a source of information (for example, a radio broadcast or a lecture) should have an alternate transcription available for viewing or download. In cases where video and audio are combined, such as music videos or movie clips, captions of the lyrics and dialogue should also be available. The WGBH National Center for Accessible Media (NCAM) has created a software package called MAGpie (Media Access Generator) that allows you to easily create captions for streaming media in Windows Media Player, QuickTime, and Real Player formats. You can download the software for free at *ncam.wgbh.org/webaccess/magpie/index.html*.

The WGBH NCAM is continuing to develop tools to aid Web accessibility. There is currently a tool in development that will allow the captioning of Flash movies. At the time this is being written, it is in beta testing, but it should soon be downloadable at the Macromedia Extension site. Also in development is CaptionKeeper, a software program that automatically strips the line-21 caption data from a TV program and feeds it to a Windows Media or Real Player encoder so that web casts of those programs can also be accessible via captions. Support for streaming text in Apple's QuickTime is also in development. As a Web designer, it's up to you to stay on top of the latest accessibility technologies such as these, and use them to make the Web a great resource for everyone.

figure | 5-21 |

You can download MAGpie for free at the WGBH National Center for Accessible Media's website *(ncam.wgbh.org/ webaccess/magpie/ index.html)*.

Physical Disabilities

Physical disabilities that restrict the movement of the arms or the dexterity of the hands require more in the way of hardware-related solutions than specialized site design. For example, a person with a severe physical disability will often use a hands-free keyboard, which is a standing box with representations of letters, numbers, and symbols that react to input from a laser-pointer that can be mounted on a hat or a pair of glasses. This is a powerful tool for typing text and navigating by the use of keyboard shortcuts or the tab key. In this case, you will help the user mightily if you label your tables in a logical sequence, as we mentioned earlier in the Blindness section. You can also use a special HTML attribute—ACCESSKEY (see Selected HTML Glossary sidebar, page 116)—to "keyboard enable" certain sections of your web page, or certain options in a form. In other words, by pressing ALT and a specific key, a user can go straight to that section or choose that particular option. When you use this attribute, make sure that you let people know which shortcut to use by underlining the appropriate letter. For example, if the text in your first cell begins "Caring for your Cat," you might underline the letter C. If the text in your second cell begins "Collars and Combs," you might underline the letter o since C is already taken. If there is no text in the cell containing a letter you can use, then just include some small, unobtrusive text that says "press 'K' for this section" or something like that.

figure **5-22**

Each element of this form was keyboard enabled using the ACCESSKEY attribute. Using this attribute does not automatically underline the shortcuts for you. You must do that manually, using the U tag.

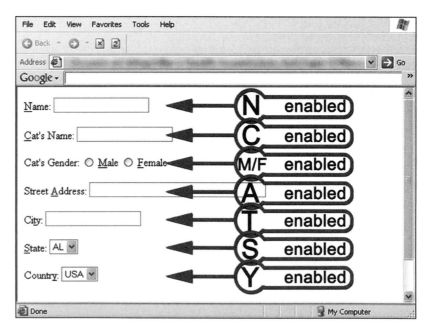

In cases where you cannot provide these options, or if the user's browser doesn't support them, remember that it requires a significant amount of effort, patience, and time to navigate a website without using quick keys. By keeping your menu structure simple, logical, and in the same place, you can make a visit to your website a much more enjoyable experience than it otherwise would be.

figure |5-24|

This is John Benson at work. He is using a hands-free keyboard (LUCY) by aiming a laser pointer attached to a pair of lensless glasses. When he runs into something that requires a mouse, he manipulates a trackball with his chin. Remember our discussion about the importance of tab order and quick keys? You can find out more about John at his website: *www.jobenwebdesigns.com.*

figure |5-25|

Here we see LUCY by herself, courtesy of Keytools, Ltd. *(www.keytools.com).* This marvelous device enables people like John who have disabilities to manipulate the computer much more easily than they otherwise could.

figure |5-23|

This is John Benson. He is a remarkable individual, and living proof that you can accomplish anything you set your mind to. Cerebral Palsy has taken away the use of his arms and legs, but John realized his dream to become a web designer anyway. Here he is graduating with an Internet Webmaster Technician Associate Degree.

John Benson is a remarkable individual, and living proof that you can accomplish anything you set your mind to. Cerebral Palsy has taken away the use of his arms and legs, but John realized his dreams of becoming a web designer anyway. Here he is graduating with an Internet Webmaster Technician Associate degree (figure 5-23).

John uses a hands-free keyboard (LUCY) by aiming a laser pointer, which is attached to a pair of lensless glasses. When he runs into something that requires a mouse, he manipulates a trackball with his chin. Remember our discussion about the importance of tab order and quick keys? You can find out more about John at his website: *www.jobenwebdesigns.com.*

LUCY is a marvelous device, which enables people like John with disabilities to manipulate the computer much easier than they otherwise could.

Using these techniques can also help those with physical disabilities that are not so debilitating, but still restrictive. For example, a person with a repetitive stress injury (RSI) in the hands and/or arms would find it painful to type on an average keyboard and especially to use a mouse. Instead, he might use a specially designed keyboard or speech recognition software and navigate using many keyboard shortcuts. So, you can see how the techniques we just discussed would benefit him, as well.

▶ HTML GLOSSARY

ACCESSKEY (attribute)

Purpose: makes a tab stop accessible by using a keyboard shortcut

Usage: inside TD tag combined with TABINDEX attribute

Example 1: accesskey used in an anchor tag

```
<A HREF="top" ACCESSKEY="T">
</A>
```

Example 2: accesskey used in a table cell *(you must use TABINDEX also)*

```
<TABLE>
<TR>
<TD TITLE="Caring for your Cat" TABINDEX=1
ACCESSKEY="C"><U>C</U>aring for your Cat
</TD>
</TR>
</TABLE>
<td tabindex=1 accesskey="k">
```

Example 3: accesskey used in a form

```
<FORM>
<LABEL FOR="name"
ACCESSKEY="N"><U>N</U>ame:
</LABEL>
<INPUT TYPE="text" TABINDEX=1 SIZE="25">
</FORM>
```

ALT (attribute)

Purpose: assigns a description to an image that can be understood by text readers, and seen when mousing over an image

Usage: inside IMG tag

Example:

```
<IMG SRC="cats.jpg" ALT="two cats sleeping">
```

TABINDEX (attribute)

Purpose: tells the TAB key where to go next

Usage: primarily inside table cells and form elements

Examples: see ACCESSKEY examples 2 and 3

TITLE (attribute)

Purpose: assigns a description to a table row or cell that can be understood by text readers, and seen when mousing over that area

Usage: primarily inside table rows and cells

Example: see ACCESSKEY example 2

Cognitive and Neurological Disabilities

It is impossible to determine exactly how many people in the United States have some form of learning disability (LD), such as dyslexia or attention deficit disorder (ADD). Between 1997 and 1998, the United States Center for Disease Control did a study of children in almost eighty thousand households, looking for signs of both LD and ADD to determine possible causal factors. The results of this study showed that three percent had a diagnosis of ADD, four percent had LD, and four percent had both ADD and LD. Even if it turned out that only one percent of the U.S. population suffered from these problems, that would still be nearly three million people. In addition to this, there are also many people who have problems related to low intelligence due to conditions like Down's Syndrome, and memory problems, such as loss of short-term memory due to trauma. All of these things should be considered when designing your site.

A person with LD or ADD can find it difficult to absorb large amounts of text, and can be easily distracted by flashy or animated graphics. A person with low intelligence or memory problems can become easily confused and lost on a website. There are three main things you can do to solve these problems. First, as we have said many times, keep your navigation and menu structure simple. Keep your menu links organized in a logical manner and keep them in the same place throughout the site. Second, whenever feasible, use graphics as a visual anchor for long strings of text. To a person who has trouble staying focused when reading, these can be as helpful as knotted handholds when climbing a rope. Third, make sure that whenever you use moving graphics or music on a site, you allow the user the option to turn it off. These things can be very distracting for someone who already finds it difficult to focus.

CHAPTER SUMMARY

Seem like a lot to digest? Maybe at first, but all it really comes down to is being thorough. Take some time to consider all the different groups of people we talked about and their needs. Formulate a strategy of design and create a checklist that includes all the details we recommended. Get in the habit of using your checklist as you go along. Pretty soon, including these features in your design will be second nature. Problems with website accessibility can end up costing companies money due to legal issues, so a good understanding of web accessibility is a valuable skill. Make sure you take the time to develop it.

THE WEB DESIGN ARTIST
AT WORK

Eric Jordan

Job Title: Co-founder, President, and Chief Creative Officer

Organization: 2Advanced Studios, LLC

Number of years in field: Eleven

Partial client list: Nintendo of America; EA Games; Warner Bros./Morgan Creek; Fujitsu; AOL; Six Flags; Oakley; Vulcan, Inc.; Bacardi Global Brands; Ford Motor Company

Professional affiliations: 2Advanced Studios, 2Advanced.net

Books co-authored: *New Masters of Flash; Flash 5 Bible; Flash MX Bible; Flash 5, Creative Web Animation*

Magazines written for: *Computer Arts, CreateOnline, DesignMag* (South America), *Impress Web Design* (South Korea), *Design Times*

Awards: Ford Focus 2005, Website WebAward, 2004 WebAwards Competition; LogoYes, Website WebAward, 2004 WebAwards Competition; *Exorcist The Beginning*, Best Movie Website WebAward, 2004 WebAward Competition; Christopher Lawrence, Outstanding Website WebAward, 2004 WebAward Competition; Favorite Website Award, LogoYes Website/application; Gold Award for V.4 Prophecy, 2004 Summit Creative Awards; Silver Award for Ford F-150, 2004 Summit Creative Awards; Silver Award for AYSO Soccer, 2004 Summit Creative Awards; and many others.

Websites: 2advanced.com, 2advanced.net

What type of work do you do at your company?

The 2Advanced team has a wide range of expertise, including: interactive design, broadcast-quality motion graphics, 3D design and illustration, sophisticated backend solutions, e-commerce, and complex content-managed systems.

What got you interested in this field?

I grew up on science fiction, electronic music, and the dawn of efficient computer technology. I wanted to pursue several creative directions; all of them were based on art. The new software for creating digital art and motion graphics channeled my focus into interactive design.

What was your first industry-related job?

Senior web designer at a local web design studio in El Toro, CA.

What prompted you to start your company?

2Advanced Studios is the result of a collective dream to work in an environment where we could set our own rules and hours, and at the same time have the ability to progressively and passionately push the new media envelope.

What type of hardware/software do you use?

To design graphics, we use Adobe Photoshop CS, Adobe Illustrator 10, and Macromedia Freehand MX. We create motion graphics with Adobe After

Effects 6.0, and use programs such as Partical-Illusion and Discreet Combustion for effects and compositing (green-screening). For 3D, we use 3D Studio Max and Cinema 4D.

Where do you find creative inspiration?

My inspiration comes from various sources: electronic music, over-imaginative daydreams/nightmares of the future, and books. For me, inspiration is more a saturation of overlapping experiences that produce a certain mindset.

What would you consider your biggest career accomplishment?

My biggest achievement would have to be building a successful web design studio that has survived an unstable economy and still inspires people all over the world.

What has been your most challenging project?

Logoyes.com was one of our most challenging projects. The client wanted an online application that would allow small-business owners to color, rotate, scale, and produce their own customized logo. We scripted tools that allowed for complex control over symbols and fonts used in the application, and that controlled the output of the file, in EPS format, for delivery to the customer. We also built a complex user voting system; users could email logos to their friends and colleagues so they could vote on their favorite. In the end, what we created for Logoyes was a breakthrough Flash application.

What qualities/skills do you look for in a potential employee?

First, we look for skill, knowledge, and versatility. We only hire people who have proven themselves in the field. Our designers and developers need to turn on a dime for the client, because that is what the client expects from us. Additionally, it takes a dedication and passion for design that makes what you do not a "job." If you are a clock watcher, 2Advanced doesn't have a place for you. Our employees are artists, and often spend long nights at their systems in "the zone" because they love what they do. They are constantly learning, and pushing themselves to see what they can accomplish.

What is the one thing you wish someone had told you before getting into this field?

"Polish up your customer service skills." Dealing with several projects and clients on a daily basis requires careful attention to project timelines in order to keep everyone happy.

What types of credentials are most important in finding a job in your field?

For our potential employees, we typically do not look for any formal credentials. With design, you either have it or you don't. I won't say that a formal design education is a bad thing, because it helps people understand why certain things work in design and why certain things don't.

How much of what you do is a collaborative effort, either between you and the client or between you and your team?

Ninety percent of our clients trust us with their projects and are not involved in the creative process. Nearly every project is an internal collaboration between the designer and the programmers. Everyone on the staff has a unique strength; we all work together to make things turn out better than the client expected.

What are your plans for the future of 2Advanced?

We are exploring the areas of video and 3D. As high-speed Internet access becomes the standard, we want to offer solutions that leverage a full range of technologies. As always, we will focus on design and functional backends, but we look forward to the creation of virtual worlds, complex interfaces, interactive applications, and media-enriched experiences. At the business level, we don't anticipate growing too much larger. We want to sustain our edge, and we never want to lay off team members. So far, we have been quite fortunate in this respect.

in review

1. In your own words, define web accessibility.

2. What is the Americans with Disabilities Act (ADA)?

3. How does the ADA apply to web design?

4. What does it mean to simplify the content of your site?

5. What does it mean to simplify the navigation of your site?

6. How many clicks should it take to get from any page to any other page in your site?

7. Name two things you can do to make your site more accessible to the visually impaired.

8. Name something you can incorporate into your design that can make your site more accessible to people with low vision, as well as people with color blindness.

9. If you have audio content on your site, what can you do to make sure people with hearing disabilities can also appreciate it?

10. What can you do to make your site more user-friendly for those who have a hard time using a mouse?

11. What three things can you do to make your site easier for a person with cognitive disabilities to use?

exercises

1. Visit the website for Bobby *(www.cast.org/bobby/)* and test three of your favorite high-profile websites for accessibility. You might be surprised at the results. For each one, write out an action plan that outlines what could be done to improve its accessibility.

2. Design a website using at least two tables with at least six cells each. Make sure you use row and column headers (the TITLE attribute). Draw out a "map" of your site that shows all tables with the row and column headers written in. Draw boxes for each image and write in the ALT tag information that you have coded into your site. Give the map to a friend and ask him or her to act as the text reader while you navigate. Now, place your fingers on the TAB and SHIFT keys (TAB to go forward, SHIFT+TAB to go backward), and close your eyes. Your friend should read the contents of each cell (beginning with the headers), and the ALT tags for each image as you navigate to them. See how well you can navigate your site without peeking.

3. Design a website with the same specifications as in exercise #2 (you can use the same one if you've already done it). Keep your eyes open this time, and try to navigate the site without using the mouse. If you can't do it, go back and redesign it until you can.

4. Design a website and keyboard enable each major section. For an extra challenge, include a form and keyboard enable each response. When you're finished, try to navigate the site without using your mouse at all.

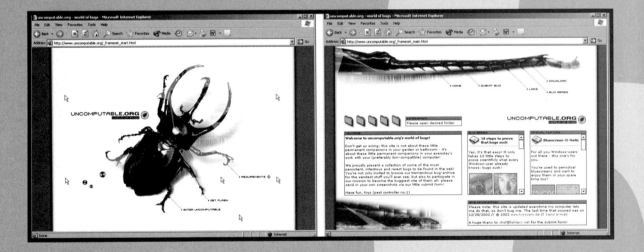

| turning your creative potential into a reality |

objectives

Identify and eliminate interruptions in your creative flow

Create your ideal work environment

Discover your personal creative process

Harness the power of themes

Put your creativity to work—develop a portfolio

Create a scope for your projects

introduction

Designing a web page is not a mechanical process—it's a creative one. A person can mechanically follow every rule in this book, and still end up with an unappealing website. Good design requires a certain artistic sense. No one is saying you have to be able to draw or paint like a master (although it doesn't hurt). What we're saying is you have to think like one. Even if you can't sketch or paint your art, you need to be able to conceptualize it. By now, you've done a fair amount of critiquing of your own work, as well as other people's. You should be starting to refine your artistic sense. In other words, you should be able to tell what looks good and what doesn't. That's all well and good when you're analyzing something in front of you. What happens when the thing in front of you is a blank computer screen, waiting for you to fill it up? You feel confident in your artistic sense. You know you can create good design; you've done it numerous times before as projects for this book. So why isn't anything coming to you? Why does your mind seem as blank as the computer screen? You are now experiencing the age-old problem of designer's anxiety. You've heard of writers having writer's block. Well, designers get it, too. In this chapter, we'll show you how to overcome this obstacle, and get your creative juices flowing.

Once you're a lean, mean creative machine, the logical next step is to find a job to channel all that creativity into. To land a good job, you really need a good portfolio. In the graphics industry this is a necessity, so we'll give you some tips for developing your portfolio. A large part of web design is freelance or contract work. Why? Many small businesses or even individuals want a website, but don't have the resources to keep a full-time web designer on staff. They are, however, willing to pay whenever they need something done, so we will also give you advice about contracting.

FINDING YOUR BEST WORK ENVIRONMENT

Do you work better alone or with a group of people? Do you find that music distracts you or helps you concentrate? Do you work better at home, or are you easily sidetracked? Does being in a more formal setting, like an office, library or school, improve your discipline? Do you need a neat and organized space, or do you feel that you're most at home in the clutter? Are you more creative during the daytime or at night? When you're on the computer, would you rather have the lights on or off? Obviously there are no right or wrong answers to these questions; they are matters of personal preference, but they are far from trivial. In order to produce your best work, you need to be able to focus on that work. Small distractions are actually big distractions if they keep you from completing your job.

Analyzing your work habits will help you to choose a setting that works best for you. There are times, however, when your setting is beyond your control. If you freelance, you can work in nearly any environment you like; if you have a notebook computer, you can even work at the library or the local coffee shop. However, if you get a job for a web design firm, or if you're the on-site webmaster for a corporation, you may find yourself in a more structured work environment. Some companies understand that artists may work best in a nontraditional setting, and are willing to accommodate their designers. Nevertheless, many of them will prefer that you work certain hours and work in the office instead of at home. They might feel more secure if they can communicate with you face-to-face on a daily basis. In this case, you should ask yourself, "How can I work best in the environment I am given?" Also realize that you may need to recondition yourself, to modify old habits or adopt new ones in order to fit into a particular work environment. For example, if you tend to maintain a disorganized workspace, you should try to change this habit to work in a corporation. If you just can't concentrate without a mess, take a photo of your messy home-office and take it to work with you.

THOUGHTS BEFORE YOU START DESIGNING

So you have a workspace, you have a client, and now you're sitting down to work. What are you supposed to design? What will this client like? Let's back up a little bit. Before you start designing, you need to have a conversation or two with the client. Ask the client to show you a some websites that have the basic style and elements they're looking for. Ask them what colors they like, and what colors represent their business. What colors will work best for their customers? For example, if your client runs a traditional beauty salon that caters mostly to senior citizens, chances are they're not looking for something with a black background, a lot of animation, and a font that resembles graffiti. Likewise, if your client is a DJ, you probably won't be designing a website that uses muted pastels and a flowing script font. You're going to have a hard time getting started on the website if you don't get a reasonably definite idea of what the client wants and who the target audience is. Keep in mind that this website represents the client, and therefore he or she will usually want a good deal of control over how the site looks. Don't be discouraged if you are left little room for creative expression. The challenge is to apply your creativity to the client's style. Put yourself in their place. It's a scary proposition to put the identity and online presence of *your* company in the hands of another person. Imagine that you're a best-selling author, and you've just optioned your novel to a big Hollywood studio that wants to turn it into a feature film. Wouldn't you want to have some control over the screenplay? If you think about it, it's not hard to understand why the client wants to be involved.

Now that you know what the client wants and who the target audience is, it's time to get to work. Take all of the information the client shared with you into consideration, but take it with a grain of salt. You are a designer, and therefore it is your job to provide the client with a great site. If they showed you a site as an example of what they want, don't just copy it exactly. The client may have a very mediocre site, or even a bad site, in mind. Design a great site anyway, keeping in mind the client's specifications, but bending these to your will. The client will most likely recognize that your work is better than what they expected.

A good example of this is the typical "rippling water" background. Most beginning designers love putting busy backgrounds on a web page. They mistakenly believe that the more graphic elements you have, the better and more impressive your web page will be. As you gain more experience, you will learn that some backgrounds are not good for readability and do not look professional. Consequently, most of us learn to hate them.

For the same reasons, clients sometimes fall in love with certain backgrounds, too. You can talk to the client about why the background is a bad idea, but the client may be convinced that that background is absolutely necessary for the site. Let's say that the client runs an aquarium business, putting together large aquarium systems for other businesses. He is convinced that a blue water background is absolutely necessary for his site, and insists that it appear somewhere on the site. Can you think of a new and creative way to incorporate this overused, tiled background into your design?

YOUR CREATIVE PROCESS AND THE BLANK SCREEN SYNDROME

What do I mean by **creative process**? A creative process is simply your personalized system of approaching a design project. In other words, it's how you keep yourself from staring in horror at a blank computer screen. Raw creativity comes and goes. One day you may wake up feeling creative. The next day, you may not. If you make your living based on your creativity, you have to find a way to call it up at will—a routine for "jumpstarting" your creative engine. Without such a system, you'll find deadlines a difficult thing to deal with. The following section demonstrates my personal creative system and how I approach my job every day.

figure | 6-1 |

Blank screen
syndrome.

First of all, it helps to realize that you don't have to come up with an earth-shattering new design concept every time. Nor do you have to produce a finished draft right up front. Creating a rough, initial *sketch* is not only acceptable, but usually preferred. Your boss doesn't want you spending unproductive hours working on finished designs that you might not use. Instead, just sketch out a few quick design schemes that you think could work, and show them to your superiors and/or clients. This can mean literally sketching them out on paper, or quickly throwing together some basic design elements and colors on the screen, whichever way works best for the situation. This is a really good way to narrow down your possibilities without wasting a lot of time.

When you first start to design, even the smallest task can seem daunting. You feel as if you're expected to turn a blank screen into a great masterpiece by pressing a few buttons. When your boss tells you the first sketch is due in four hours, the situation becomes worse. When I first started out, I was scared for two years straight! I avoided my bosses because every time I saw them, they were asking me for a new sketch. Now I love to sketch and I'm very good at it. I just had to get over my fear of failure.

So how do you defeat the blank screen and get over your fears of design? It's actually pretty simple. Here's the way I approach the creative process for web design. The first thing I do to overcome a blank screen is to put the client's logo on it. In most cases, the emphasis of the website is the logo anyway. Also in most cases, the client has already chosen a certain color scheme. Your color design should reflect that scheme. By this I mean, the colors used in the logo should match the colors in your design. So there you go. With just a couple of clicks, you already have the major element of the page, and have identified the color scheme. That's what I call progress.

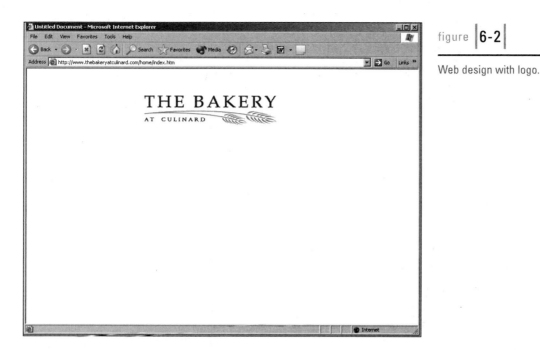

figure |6-2|

Web design with logo.

The next major part of the site is the navigation. The first thing I do to design the navigation is to write out all links and place them on the sketch. After seeing the navigation laid out in front of me, I can change and modify until it looks right. The important thing is just to get it on the screen. Not too much—just the essentials. Remember, keep the navigation simple and your site will be easier to use.

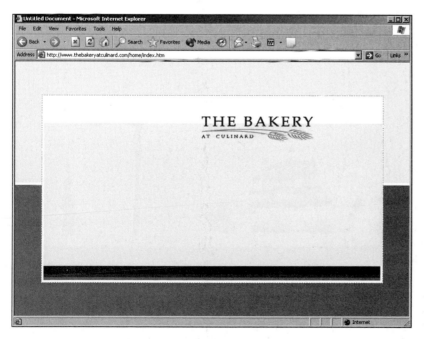

figure |6-3|

Web design with logo and colors.

figure | 6-4 |

Web design with logo,
colors, and navigation.

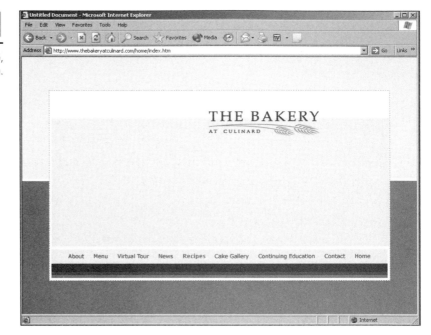

Now, stop and think about what we've done. In less than an hour, we've
narrowed down our design options from infinity to ... well, a whole lot less
than that. You have the major elements, the color scheme, and the
navigation all nailed down. So what's left? Not much. Now you just have to
come up with a few graphical elements, unify them into a theme that can
be applied to the entire site, and add to the basics until the client is happy.

figure | 6-5 |

Finished web design.

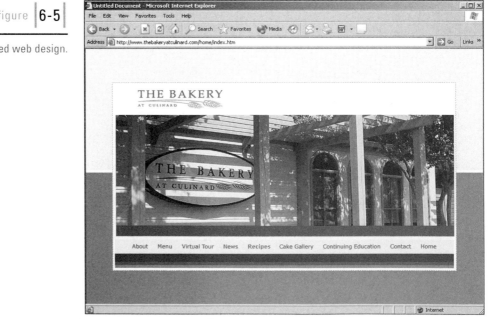

Whether you decide to use my creative process or develop your own, remember to lay out all the basic elements first. This is key because it will establish your work parameters right up front, and prevent you from veering off in the wrong direction. Time is money, and a blank screen waits for no one.

WEBSITE THEMES

Most award-winning websites are built around one simple, major element, idea, or concept. In other words, they have a **theme**. Having a theme for your site is an easy way to make it interesting and give it some kind of meaning that your users can identify with. Let's say you have a client who owns a restaurant built into an old steamboat. Because of the age of the boat, the client wants the design to appear like the site was made in 1912. And you should already know from your history classes what websites looked like back then. Seriously though, when you think of early twentieth-century photographs, you think faded, scratched, cracked, curling, sepia-tone photos. That becomes the theme of the site. Of course, you wouldn't want to overly distress the photos to the point that they're unrecognizable. Any theme should leave room for practical considerations.

Now, if you were simply told to design a site for a steamboat restaurant, at first you might not really be sure what a steamboat site should look like. But with the suggestion of the old 1912 styling, my head starts spinning with ideas. How about yours? Can you imagine the endless visual possibilities? This is the power behind a theme. It can focus your creative power and provide a framework for your design scheme.

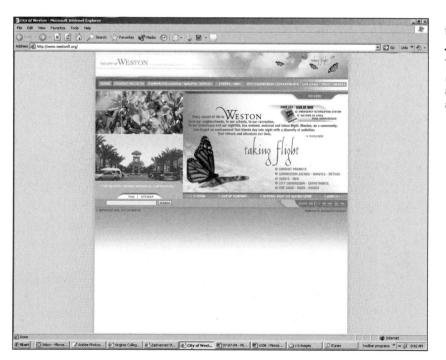

figure | 6-6 |

The website for Westin, Florida *(www.westonfl.org)* uses butterflies and great color schemes to create an amazing experience.

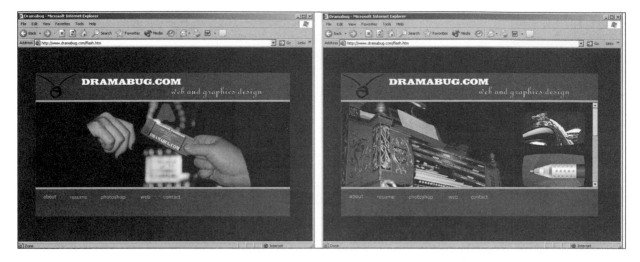

figure 6-7

Dramabug.com uses an old-time theater approach to the website.

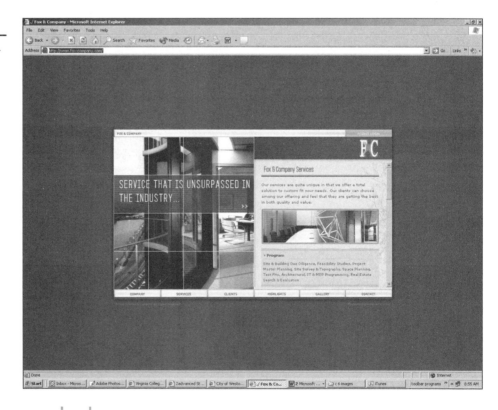

figure 6-8

The Fox & Company website *(www.fox-company.com)* uses fading images and great color.

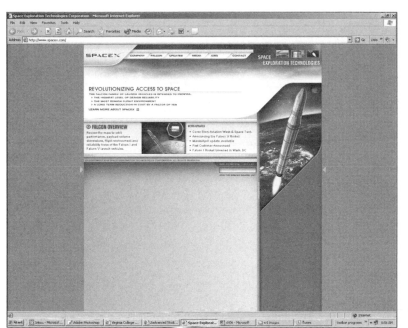

figure |6-9|

SpaceX.com uses a space theme and ties it together with a saturated color.

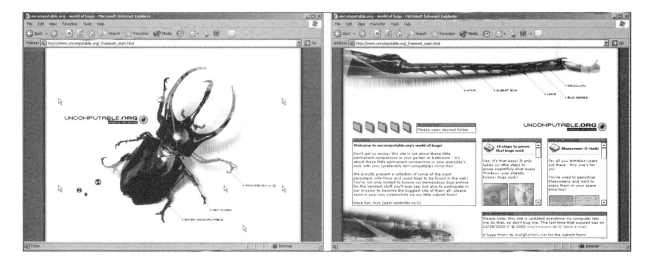

figure |6-10|

Uncomputable.org uses a bug theme to illustrate computer bugs. It really makes the site stand out as a very creative approach to web design.

MAINTAINING THE CREATIVE MACHINE

michael sickinger

Michael Sickinger, an accomplished graphic designer, is art director of the Creative Marketing Studio at Firmenich, a fragrance company. Michael also frequents colleges and universities, speaking to students about working in the field of graphic design.

Maintaining the creative machine means exactly that—creativity needs constant maintenance to keep running at maximum potential. Creativity must be fed with anything and everything you can get your hands, eyes, and mind on. Tools to keep your thoughts clean and running strong are everywhere; you just need to know how and where to find them.

Having a keen eye is the key to properly maintaining a strong creative mind. A sharp eye will catch all that is around to be seen. Give yourself a new perspective and try to look at things differently. Use your eyes and mind together to see more than just what is there. This not only has you looking for visuals in a more innovative light, but also gives the eyes and mind a good creative workout.

• Keep your eyes peeled when watching television, a movie, or surfing the Web. Leisurely paying attention to graphics will build your creative toolbox with items that could be needed at a later date. Notice how things are laid out, how they animate, if the font matches the mood, and most of all, think to yourself: how can I do that?

• A finely tuned creative engine is always upgrading to something newer and faster; don't become last year's model! One thing that's good, and bad, about a career in visual communications is that it's constantly evolving. Computers have revolutionized the industry, and change happens almost every day. In order to be competitive you must stay up to date with technology and learn as much as you can as fast as you can. There are always things to be learned; don't fall behind and let technology pass you by.

• Another important maintenance procedure for creativity is to keep in tune with the design of the times. Just like computers, design changes over time. An ad created in the early 90s probably won't look as cutting edge during the present. Keep those creative gears greased with current design technique and style in order to keep your creativity looking shiny and new.

• As with any mechanical device, there are things that can keep the device from working properly—inhibitors. Creativity works the same way. Having something on your mind while trying to be creative is like a pebble caught in a cog; there's something in the way of it functioning correctly. If you're too busy thinking about what happened yesterday, you're not going to be able to focus on what you have to do today. Take a walk, have some coffee, or listen to a good CD. Clear your head and get those creative spark plugs crackling.

A machine will break down and cease to operate if not maintained on a routine basis. Creativity will do the same. In order to keep creativity fresh and exciting, you must be willing to give it what it needs. Keep your creativity on the cutting edge by constantly feeding it with new visuals, technology, up-to-date design exposure, and stay away from creative inhibitors. Keep these things in mind, and your creativity will be running at maximum potential.

DEVELOPING YOUR PORTFOLIO

All right, now that you know how to consolidate your creative powers and technical training into a productive process, what's the next step? Finding a job, of course. In the world of graphic design, the most essential step toward getting work is creating a portfolio. You could have a Ph.D. in web design, but that doesn't mean a thing without a portfolio. In this field, you are only as good as the work you've done. To show it off, you should maintain both a hard copy and an online portfolio.

figure | 6-11 |

A typical portfolio case.

figure | 6-12 |

A brushed metal portfolio case.

Portfolio Formats

For your hard copy, use either a relatively nice binder and keep your work in plastic sheeting, or some kind of small carrying case and adhere your work to pieces of mounting board that fit neatly inside. You can get creative with the display, but make sure it still has an air of professionalism. Never, never, never carry disorganized loose sheets of paper to an interview.

You should also have an online version that can be easily accessed by any potential client or employer. In fact, you should put the web address on your resume and business cards. Can you believe that I have personally interviewed web designers who did not have an online portfolio? How is a web designer going to get a job without a website? Your portfolio site itself will be the largest part of your portfolio. If you don't do a good job designing your own site, no one will think you can do a good job for them, either. Remember the old adage "You never get a second chance to make a first impression." I recommend that in addition to your portfolio gallery, you also have a resume and an "about" section where you can add those details you couldn't put in your resume. Speaking of details in your resume, you might want to remove specific personal information like your phone number or street address. You should definitely include a contact link, but just be cautious about putting personal information on the Web for everyone to see.

What Most Companies Are Looking For

When it comes to web design positions, most companies are looking to hire someone that they don't have to manage. In other words, they're looking for self-motivated and self-disciplined people who can solve problems and multitask. As the web design market becomes more saturated, companies are looking for designers with a wider range of skills. If you're a web designer, companies may also expect you to be a graphic designer (in other words, to design flyers, brochures, etc.). If you're a web programmer, a company may want you to also know how to create and manage a database. This is good news for those who are willing to go the extra mile to develop a complete skill set. Those who are looking to put forth minimal effort and learn only what they need to get by may find themselves left behind. The more skills you have, the better your chances are of landing a good job.

The Importance of Presentation

There is a certain stereotype that represents members of the artistic community as traditionally having unkempt hair, torn and faded clothes, visible tattoos, and/or multiple facial piercings. In many cases, this may be accurate, but corporate America is a different story. That kind of presentation might work if you were a newly discovered artist being displayed at a trendy gallery opening in New York or L.A., but it won't work in an office building. What you have to realize is that the majority of your clients probably won't be rock bands and alternative culture magazines; they'll be pharmacies, churches, family-oriented product labels, financial institutions, and the like. Presentation means everything in this market. You can have a great portfolio, but if you show up in jeans, and the copies of your work are crumpled or bent, you may not get the job.

No one is trying to change your identity. We're not saying you can't have a certain hairstyle, or tattoos, or even piercings. What we're saying is that you need to understand the conventions of the traditional business environment and comply with them during business hours. So comb your hair neatly, pay attention to personal hygiene, dress nicely, wear something that covers up those tattoos, and take out the eyebrow ring. It's not selling out, it's just smart business. You have to understand that you're not doing the clients a favor by agreeing to design their websites. They can easily find someone else to do the job. *You* have to convince *them* that you're the right person for the job. That means coming across as a responsible, experienced professional. You can argue all day long that appearance doesn't necessarily reflect work ethic and professional habits, and you'd be right, but it won't make any difference to the client. There is a certain level of decorum in place, and that's just the way it is. You must find a way to adapt your personal style to it.

What Should Be in Your Portfolio?

The more skills shown in your portfolio, the better the chance that you'll get a job. Traditional art skills are always a big plus in this field. As mentioned before, you may be expected to function as a graphic designer, as well. If not, it's still great if you can create your own web graphics from scratch. Being able to sketch ideas out on paper can improve communication with both clients and supervisors. If you possess these skills, make sure a potential employer knows it. If you can draw freehand or paint, if you have an eye for photography, digital imaging, illustration, graphic design, and more, put a few pieces in your portfolio. Let me qualify that statement by saying that if you include traditional artwork, make sure it's tasteful and professional. Limit cartoon or comic book characters (unless it directly relates to the job you're applying for), and certainly include nothing explicit, gory, or death-themed. If you're more technical-minded and have some programming skills, make sure you include links to sites you've programmed and examples of your code.

Of course, when you're seeking a position as a web designer, the primary element in your portfolio should be screen captures of sites you've designed. This doesn't mean you need to include every single page you've ever designed in your life. This should be a collection of the absolute best—a "greatest hits" album. You may be thinking that, if you included everything you ever designed, there would only be five or six pages. What do you do about that? The answer is simple: design more! That may sound a little harsh, but you have to look at it from the employer's point of view. Why would they hire someone who can only show them two or three good designs and two or three mediocre ones, when there are plenty of applicants with a portfolio full of their best work? Building a good portfolio takes time, but it's definitely worth it.

On a more technical note, it's a good idea to capture your designs from within a web browser. This demonstrates that the website is (or at least was) *live*. In other words, it has been published online. It's also a good idea to include several copies of your resume. That way you can leave one with your interviewer and still have copies to give out to other potentially interested parties. Overall, try to keep the total amount of pages (excluding multiple copies of your resume) between ten and fifteen.

Be Original and Creative

Now that I am in a position to hire people, I get very bored with the typical black leather portfolio case. My eyes light up when I see a creative, nontypical portfolio. The case I'm currently using is made out of brushed metal and really makes a serious statement when I go to an interview. My suggestion is to find books about portfolios and research creative portfolios on the Web. You can even create your own case if you think you can do it well. If you elect this last option, however, be honest with yourself about how it looks. If your end result includes glitter and sequins, you should probably go back to the black leather case.

Don't be afraid to draw inspiration from other sources. It's been said that no one ever produces anything truly original, that we all unconsciously plagiarize things that we don't distinctly remember, but which have made an impression on us in the past. This may or may not be true, but my point is that being influenced by someone else's style is not the same thing as copying it. You never want to make an exact copy of someone else's style, but you can really spark your own creativity by looking at other designers' work. The following websites are all web portfolios; use them for inspiration.

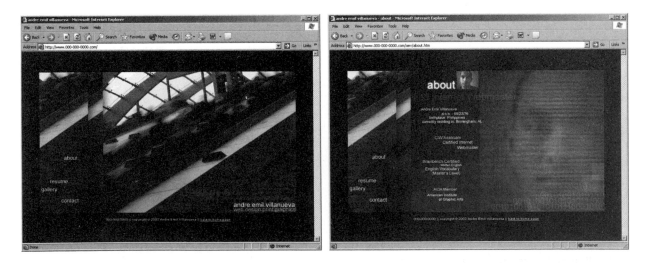

figure |6-13|

The portfolio of Andre Villanueva
(www.000-000-0000.com).

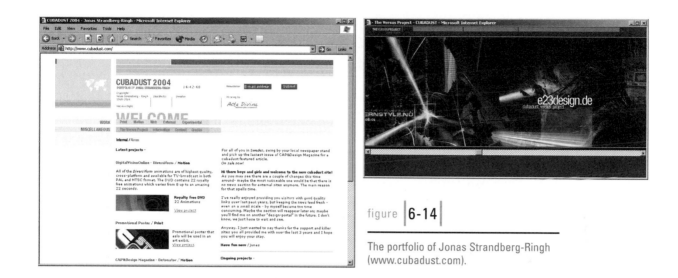

figure | 6-14 |

The portfolio of Jonas Strandberg-Ringh
(www.cubadust.com).

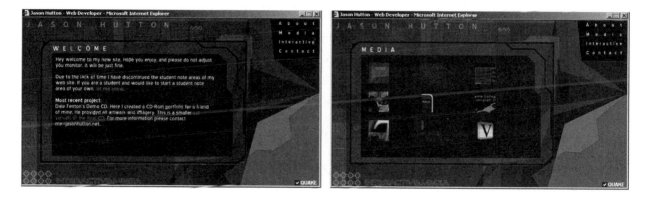

figure | 6-15 |

The portfolio of Jason Hutton
(www.jasonhutton.net).

SCOPE

So you've awakened your creative processes, designed a portfolio, and used it to get a contract job. You're ready to dive right in and start working, right? Not just yet. Once you begin to design professionally, you take on a whole new level of responsibility. There are certain things the client needs from you, and certain things you need from the client. In these situations, a verbal agreement just doesn't cut it. It doesn't matter if you're designing your church's website for free or if you're being paid to design your dry cleaner's site, you need to establish a *scope* before you start the site. A **scope** is a statement of precisely what you plan to do for the company and at what price. This statement is signed by both parties and tells the client in black and white everything that you plan to do for them. It also sets a price for any additional work that may creep up later. Usually called *scope creep*, this is an important issue and should not be left out. You never know when unforeseen circumstances will add to your workload, and you need to make sure you'll be adequately compensated. Not only that, but as you calculate the amount of time it will take you to design, you assume that the client will freely provide you with all the information you need to do so. You'll quickly discover that not every client is able to meet his own deadline. He may expect you to design a site in a week, but never provide you with any of the text for the site. Things like that should be included as conditions in the scope agreement.

Is a written scope really necessary? Look at it this way, when you agree to design a site, you have a certain idea of what all that entails, but the client may have a very different idea. You may think you're being hired to design an interface and add a few pictures to it. They may expect you to do all that, as well as create a new logo for them, set up a database and a shopping cart, and maintain the site for an indefinite period—all at the original price you quoted them. You can see how a lack of communication can lead to some disastrous results. Whether through confusion or sometimes through pure meanness, companies tend to take advantage of web design firms and especially freelance designers. Without some type of written agreement, you may be stuck doing ten times more work than you quoted, for fear of being sued. Creating the scope at the outset eliminates any potential confusion. Also, if your clients change their minds later and want more than you originally agreed to, that's considered outside the scope and will be billed at the rate specified in the original scope agreement.

You may think this is starting to sound complicated. It doesn't necessarily have to be. I have seen scopes that were forty-five pages long and scopes that were only fifteen words. The more complex a site, the more detailed the scope must be to avoid confusion. It's all relative to your project. If it seems like you're getting out of your depth when creating a scope, don't hesitate to contact a lawyer. In fact, you should always consult a lawyer when dealing with any type of contract. Don't feel like you're going to offend your client; this is a standard business practice. Your client wouldn't hesitate to contact his lawyer if your positions were reversed.

The following scope is a very simple form that has proven to be effective for me. I am providing it here for you as an example, not as anything authoritative. Let me say again that *you should always consult a lawyer before dealing with any type of contract.*

SCOPE

[Your company's name here] will create an up to a twelve-page brochure website to help with marketing efforts. The website will have a content management system (CMS) on every page so **[Client's name here]** can update and maintain their own content.

The scope shows what **[Client's name here]** proposes.

- Twelve hours for design, scanning, imaging, conception, photography

- Two hours for preproduction meetings, talking with client

- Six hours for setting up the CMS and form (which includes up to twelve pages of CMS)

- Custom design matching current marketing and branding standards

WEB DESIGN QUOTE

Twenty hours at $80 per hour

$1,600 total with no hidden fees

- 50 percent up front

- 50 percent when complete

- Quote does not include hosting

- Quote is based on client providing text for every page

After site is complete and approved by client, any additional changes will be considered Scope Creep and will be billed at $80 per hour.

Company name_____

Client _____

CHAPTER SUMMARY

Your creative process must be just that—*your* creative process. Elements of my own creative process have been described for you as a place to start, but you must use these as a springboard to find the methods that work best for you. Just remember as you start to design that something is better than nothing. Don't waste time staring at a blank screen. Get something up there. Once you feel confident in your ability to exercise your creativity at will, it's time to step into the market. Put together the best portfolio you can and get out there. As soon as your portfolio hooks a client, make sure that you take control from the beginning. Always use a written scope agreement to keep information flowing and prevent yourself from being taken advantage of.

in review

1. In your own words, explain why having a creative process is important to a designer.

2. What is the power of a theme?

3. Why should you have a portfolio?

4. Why should you have a hard copy of your Web work?

5. What is the blank screen syndrome?

6. Why would you lay out the basic elements of a website before you start designing?

7. In your own words, explain what a scope is.

8. When you created any type of artwork in the past, what was the creative process you used? Based on what you learned in this chapter, how can you improve on your process?

exercises

1. Surf the Web and find five themed websites. List the theme of each site, and write negative and positive comments on each theme.

2. Write a portfolio plan for yourself. Take inventory of all the pieces of work you currently have for your portfolio. Write out ideas for other portfolio pieces and set a date for your portfolio to be done.

the technologies of multimedia and web design

objectives

introduction

Let's start with the basics. What exactly is **multimedia**? Well, *media* is the plural for *medium*, which refers to a method of information delivery, or the way it is delivered. Multimedia means that information is being delivered by more than one medium at a time. Think of watching a DVD with the subtitles turned on. You can see the movie, hear the dialogue, and read it all at the same time.

This chapter is more about general technology information than specific design principles. By the time you reach this point, you should have a good understanding of how to design—and are raring to go—so this part is about launching you in the right direction. I can't stress enough how important it is to keep up with the latest technological developments relating to the Web. New developments occur every day. Anyone who has bought a brand new, top-of-the-line computer knows how fast they become yesterday's news. Pay $2,500 today, pay $750 for the same thing a month and a half from now. Computer technology evolves quickly. That's just the nature of the beast. It's tough to keep on top of things, but if you want to be a serious web designer, you'd better be up to the challenge. The more you understand about new technology, the more you can utilize it to its full potential and stay on the cutting edge.

THE TECHNOLOGIES OF MULTIMEDIA AND WEB DESIGN

figure |7-1|

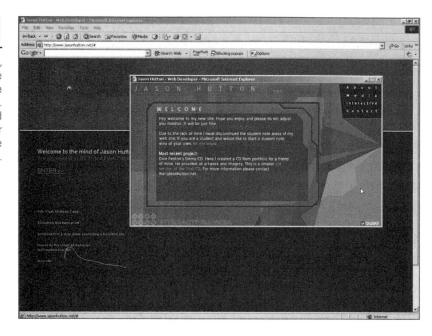

Although you can't tell from this image, this Macromedia ® Flash ™ interface quakes and flashes as you click on the links (www.jasonhutton.net). Notice that the designer has provided a checkbox in the lower right corner to disable the effect, should it become too much for you. ©2004 Jason Hutton.

DIAL-UP AND HIGH-SPEED DIAL-UP

56K dial-up modems come with almost every preassembled computer you can buy today. Not only that, but you can buy one now for around $10-$15, so there's really no point in talking about anything slower. So, what does the *K* mean? The K is short for Kbps, which in turn is short for **kilobits per second.** The most common mistake people make with Kbps is to think the Kb stands for **kilobyte**. There is actually a big difference. A *bit* is just a single binary number—a 1 or a 0—in the language of computers. A **byte** is a collection of eight bits. The prefix kilo means 1,000, although when discussing bits and bytes it actually means 1,024. So a kilobyte (KB—with an uppercase B) is eight times more data than a **kilobit** (Kb with a lowercase b). So if you're expecting your modem to deliver download speeds of 56 KB per second, you'll be very disappointed when what you get is 56 Kb per second. Actually, you won't even get that. The FCC (Federal Communications Commission) has set restrictions on 56K modems that won't allow them to go faster than 53K. On top of that, there are all kinds of other things we won't bother to go into that can interfere with your connection and lower your speed. You may be saying, "I understand what you're saying about this kilobit business, but it doesn't really mean anything to me." To see how these data rates translate into actual time, take a look at table 7-1. Just understand that these are maximum speeds. The actual speeds and wait times can vary significantly.

Type of Connection	Approx. Maximum Connection Speed	Time to Download 1 MB (theoretical)
56K Dial-Up	56,000 bps	2.4 minutes
128K ISDN	128,000 bps	1.1 minutes
Cable (standard)	3,000,000 bps	3 seconds
DSL (standard)	1,500,000 bps	5.6 seconds
Satellite	500,000 bps	16 seconds
11 Mbps Wi-Fi	11,000,000 bps	0.8 seconds

table | 7-1 |

Connection speed and time to download for different types of connections.

Lately, there have been many ISPs (Internet Service Providers) advertising software that makes your ordinary dial-up connection run up to five times faster. Could this be true? What about the FCC restrictions we just discussed? Well, it is true and it isn't. Your modem will not run any faster, no matter what. Even if it could, it would be illegal to do so. What this software actually does is **compress** the information that is delivered to your modem and to improve your browser's cache. A **cache** is a library of images that have been downloaded from web pages and stored to your hard drive. If you revisit the same page again, the computer can quickly pull up those images from your hard drive instead of downloading them again. The problem with this technology is that graphics on the Web are compressed already. Recompressing them can often yield less than satisfactory results. However, using the Internet is all about finding a balance between quality and speed. If you prefer speed to quality, and don't have access to a broadband connection, this can be your solution.

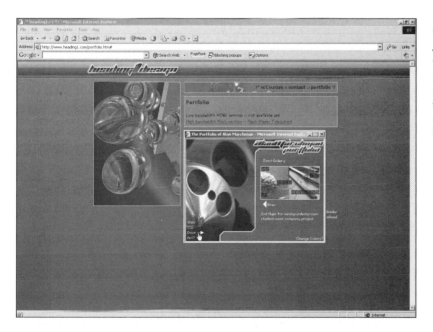

figure | 7-2 |

This site *(www.heading1.com)* also makes use of interactive Flash graphics to attract and interest users. Panels slide in from outside the screen, buttons flash, and the user can change the color of the interface. ©2004 Alan Marchman.

Another dial-up option is to have an ISDN (Integrated Services Digital Network) line installed. This is a digital phone line (as opposed to an ordinary, or **analog**, phone line), and has to be specially installed by your local phone company. They're not cheap, but do have the capacity to deliver speeds of up to 128K. Will you always get that speed? No. But then again, no type of Internet connection really carries a consistent speed.

BROADBAND CONNECTIONS

The World Wide Web, as we have discussed, is primarily a visual medium. In the beginning, waaaay back in the late 1980s and early 1990s, it delivered only text. Why? Because text can be transferred faster than anything else. Why is that true, you ask? Think back to the last time you played Pictionary. One of your teammates rolled the dice and landed on that *difficult* category. You drew the card, and the word was "improvise." How many times before the hourglass ran out did you furiously tap the paper with your pencil and wish you could just write out the word? You already knew how to spell "improvise," but you had no idea how to draw it. All right, what if a little green alien that only you can see and hear suddenly appears over your left shoulder and describes to you the perfect way to convey the term "improvise" visually. You begin furiously drawing, and sure enough, just before the timer runs out, someone guesses it. But wouldn't the whole thing have gone so much quicker if you could just write out the word? Of course, but it wouldn't be much of a game. Now, getting back on track, your computer already knows how to display characters. When you log onto the Internet looking for information, your computer connects to another computer. The other computer says, "Hey, the word you're looking for is improvise." Your computer says, "Gee, thanks," and types it on your screen. But what if that other computer starts to give your computer instructions on how to draw an image representing "improvise"? Your computer is no artist. It has no idea how to improvise. The other computer has to tell it how to draw the image, pixel by pixel. That can turn out to be a lot of information.

Now you may say, "Wait a minute. Haven't you been telling us to use images all along?" Yes, of course. No one is saying don't use images. It's just that images include a lot more information than plain text, and so take longer to download. When you get into audio and video, you're talking *a lot* more information, and even longer download times. There was a time when it just wasn't practical to try to download all that information. Many of you may not remember modems any slower than a 56K, but trust me, there were. But those days are over. Almost everyone has a 56K modem now, which provides the fastest download speeds you can get on a conventional phone line. Images are not as much of a problem now (notice I said *as much*—you still need to make them as small as possible). These days, however, we can go even further. Enter *broadband*. With a broadband connection, you can get download speeds that make your 56K seem like a relic.

Broadband means you have more **bandwidth** than with an ordinary phone line. What is bandwidth? Basically, it just means the rate of data transfer or the amount of data you can transfer in a certain period of time. If you buy a smoothie and drink it through a straw, the rate of smoothie transferred to your mouth per second is pretty low. If you pull off the lid and gulp it straight out of the cup, the rate of smoothie transfer is pretty high. An ordinary phone line is like drinking with the straw: low bandwidth. Broadband is like drinking from the cup: high bandwidth. So, now that we have broadband connections available, what are we going to do with all this extra bandwidth? Multimedia, baby.

Cable and DSL

There are three major forms of broadband connections for consumers. Cable and DSL (Digital Subscriber Line) are the most common (we'll get to the third shortly). Both of these represent "always-on" connections, which means you don't have to dial in to connect. Both use their own modems to receive and transmit signals that don't require a standard phone line. Both of them also deliver speeds many times faster than standard dial-up. As a general rule, cable modems are faster—theoretically, that is. In practice, that may or may not be true. DSL is a dedicated line between you and the phone company. It may not be capable of the same speeds a cable modem is, but you're the only one using it. Cable access, on the other hand, is shared by all the people around you who are also on the service. The more people who use it simultaneously, the less bandwidth there is to go around. As a result, your transfer rates go down. Each has its pros and cons, but for home users, they represent the best solution for high-speed Internet access.

Satellite

The third major form of consumer-level broadband connection is satellite. The transfer rates offered by satellite can rival those of cable. However, there is a certain lag time associated with the signal flying all the way to the satellite and bouncing back to your house that makes things like fast-paced Internet gaming and videoconferencing difficult. There are also a few more drawbacks. Just like cable, your satellite bandwidth can be affected by other users in the area. Unfortunately, satellite is also affected by inclement weather. If the signal can't get through the storm, you can't use the Internet. Obviously, you also need to have a dish installed. This usually isn't cheap. You can install a one-way system yourself, but two-way systems must be installed professionally, according to FCC regulations (we'll discuss the difference in a moment). This can add to the cost. The good news is, after you make it through the initial setup fees and cost of equipment, the monthly charges are competitive with cable and DSL. Even better is that satellite is available almost anywhere. You just have to be able to point the dish at the right satellite without obstruction. For people in rural areas, this is often the only option for a broadband connection.

There are two kinds of satellite service: one-way and two-way. One-way systems use a satellite modem to receive incoming data and a traditional dial-up modem to transmit. So basically, it still ties up your phone line. Download speeds can be very fast, but upload speeds are extremely slow. Two-way satellite uses the satellite modem for both receiving and transmitting. These cost a bit more, but if you do a lot of uploading or don't want to pay for a second phone line, this may sound good.

Wireless Internet

High-speed wireless Internet, or Wi-Fi, is definitely an up-and-coming technology. This is not to be confused with the WAP (Wireless Application Protocol) technology that many wireless phones have today. Signing onto the Internet via a cell phone is a great idea for basic information, but you probably won't get a better speed than you would with a standard dial-up modem. Wi-Fi is a different story. There are already companies setting up Wi-Fi "hotspots" all over the country that allow transfer rates of up to 11Mbps. That's about 200 times faster than a 56K modem! In fact, a wireless provider in California set up a structure to offer Wi-Fi access to an entire California suburb. This kind of thing is coming, and coming fast. You can be ready for it by exploring all the exciting new design elements broadband makes possible.

Naturally there are other ways to connect to the Internet than those mentioned above. We didn't even get into the industrial strength connections that many businesses use. But that's not what this chapter is about. We want to give you a taste of the possibilities, and start your mind racing to discover new ways to realize the creative potential of the Web.

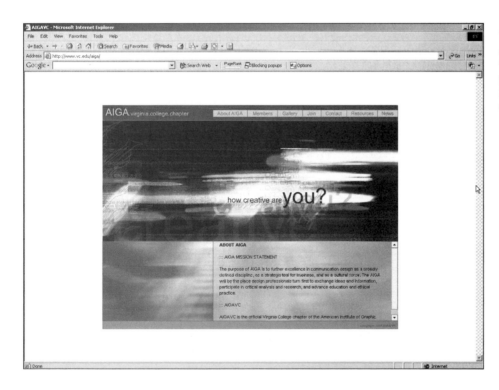

figure | 7-3 |

This site combines Flash interactivity with stunningly beautiful text art.
©2004 Andre Villanueva.

THE ANSWER LIES IN THE QUESTION

richard wilde

Richard Wilde is the chair of the graphic design and advertising departments at the School of Visual Arts in New York City. Richard is also an accomplished author and a member of HOW magazine's Editorial Advisory Board.

Whenever you embark upon solving a visual communication problem, you fall prey to the usual response of looking for the answer. This response is a habitual knee-jerk reaction, which is the great pitfall of creative thinking and leads to hackneyed solutions that reside in the known. Because if you look for answers, you are mining the area of the brain for what you already know and that in itself negates the creative act.

Curiously enough, if you move in the opposite direction and look for questions instead of answers, your possibilities can take root. It is here where new and innovative solutions arise, yet resistance to finding the appropriate question lies in the fear of moving into the unknown. We are uncomfortable in this area. Fear of failure looms over us. We are at the mercy of wanting immediate results, which the realm of answers provides.

Finding a meaningful question that ignites interest creates the condition that permits new solutions to arise. In essence, moving into a state of questioning is where creativity can flourish. This, in turn, leads to wonder, a state of openness in which new ideas take form. To wonder is our birthright, and very young children enjoy this capacity. The condition of wonder—not knowing, playing, fooling around, and looking with an open mind—is the key to problem solving, for it allows solutions to simply present themselves.

A period of pondering, reflection, introspection, and digestion allows the subconscious to make new connections and, hence, original concepts. The greater the priority a question takes, the greater the possibilities. A burning question is fueled by your emotions.

When problem solving, you might suffer from the habit of daydreaming and fantasizing. It takes discipline to simply keep your attention on a given problem, to struggle to be present in the moment using questioning as your anchor. This is a most difficult task.

Don't waste time. Cut to the chase. Probe the problem. Ask questions. Ask more questions. Let questions arise in you. Be diligent. Be merciless. Be serious. Research the problem with a questioning mind. Embrace the process, for it is the struggle of questioning that will feed you, nourish you, and make the activity of being a visual communicator truly worthwhile.

In the executional stage, questioning must again be brought in on all decisions concerning color, scale, texture, cropping, composition, tension, rhythm, space, and any other aspects concerning form. For example: the overriding concept might dictate a specific background color. However, what should the intensity be? Should the color be flat? Does it need texture? Should it move from light to dark? Does it work with the rest of the composition? Is the shape of interest? Is the composition too fussy? Is it unresolved? Feel each question. Sense each question. This is where the key lies. It is here where your search unfolds.

To be creative, you must continually struggle against your habitual nature and use the impulse of looking for answers as a warning to move in the opposite direction. The answer can always be found in the question. So ask. And ask. And ask.

VIDEO AND AUDIO ON THE WEB

I remember the first video I ever watched on the computer. It was a music video. Weezer's *Say it Ain't So,* to be specific. It was part of the "goodies" on my Windows 95 CD. Up to that point I had been used to seeing nothing but very blocky, pixelated graphics on my computer screen. The quality of the video was pretty bad compared to what I would have seen on my television, but I was astonished to be watching it on my computer. Of course, at that time I had a 14.4K modem, so watching anything like that over the Internet would have been impossible.

Even back then, people were striving to add something more than just simple graphics and text to their pages. Since receiving video was currently beyond the average user's means, they settled for audio. Much as radio came before television, audio made it to the World Wide Web before video. Although the first appearance of audio on the Web was less than satisfactory, today we have the technology to deliver flawless recordings in real time. Audio can be a powerful element in your design. It can work with your layout and graphics to create exactly the kind of mood you wish to evoke in your users. Just be aware that it can also sometimes be a distraction. Anytime you include audio in your design, make sure that if it doesn't simply fade out after a few seconds, you give the user the option (and by option, I mean a clearly marked button) to turn it off, especially if you also have viewable video content that has its own audio stream attached to it. You don't want two audio streams playing simultaneously.

Video is becoming more and more integrated into the Web. There are many sites that offer downloadable video content, as well as streaming video that you can watch in real time. Not only that, but some sites now include video demonstrations as a part of their interface.

MIDI Files

Not as common today as they once were, MIDI (Musical Instrument Digital Interface) files are really more like computerized sheet music than audio files. They provide instructions for your computer to play digital sound, which is why they're so small and can be easily transferred over the Internet. You can always recognize MIDI music by its sharp, electronic sound—kind of like a synthesizer keyboard set to a basic "electronic piano" setting. You will still find these used on amateur web pages as annoying background music, but that's about all. It's best to steer clear of these in your professional design, because they sound like a poor imitation of a song. Now that we have the technology to transmit actual songs in real time, there's no reason to settle for the next best thing.

figure | 7-4

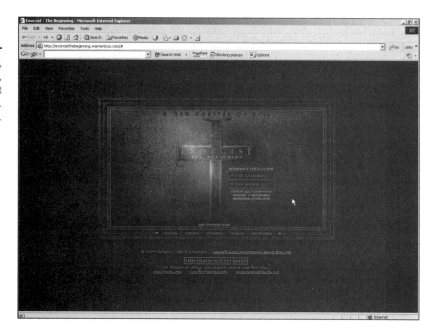

This site *(www.exorcistthebeginning.com)*, developed by 2Advanced Studios, LLC, takes full advantage of Flash in almost every way to promote this frightening film. ©2004 Morgan Creek Productions.

figure | 7-5

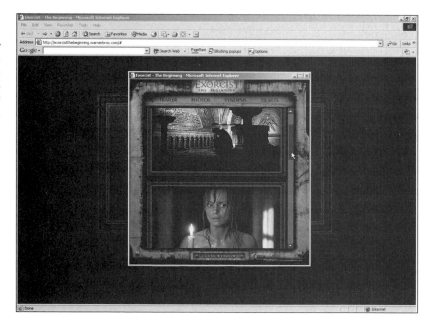

Movie trailers and eerie slideshows are just a few of the possibilities to explore *(www.exorcistthebeginning.com)*. ©2004 Morgan Creek Productions, Developed by 2Advanced Studios.

figure 7-6

Also available on this site
(www.exorcistthebeginning.com) is an
interactive Flash game, giving users the
opportunity to piece together clues and
unlock a secret area. ©2004 Morgan
Creek Productions. Developed by
2Advanced Studios.

Streaming Video and Audio

Streaming audio/video content began to emerge in 1995. Basically, it involves breaking down the audio or video file into small bite-sized chunks. The size depends on your connection speed, but ideally, each small packet will be fully downloaded just in time for your computer to play it.

Earlier in this book, we discussed image compression as finding a balance between the smallest file size and the best quality. The smaller your file size is, the quicker someone can download and view it, but the worse the image will look. The same principle applies to both audio and video. They must both be compressed for the Web in order to stream in real time. Again, you must find a balance between file size and quality. Any software package that allows you to author multimedia content into one of the standard streaming media formats will have several choices of presets that will automatically choose the optimal settings for whatever connection speed you decide. Many websites that offer streaming content also offer three or four versions of the same file with varying levels of quality to better service a wide range of users. If your multimedia content is an integral part of your interface, instead of something that must be clicked on to be activated, you should also consider making a "stripped down" alternative version of your site available for users with slower connections speeds. If you don't, you could risk turning away potential visitors to your site.

THE WEB DESIGN ARTIST
AT WORK

Colin Smith

Job Title: Owner

Organization: PhotoshopCAFE.com

Number of years in field: Eleven

Partial client list: Toyo Tires, McGraw Hill, Maxima USA, Halaki Films, Velocity Entertainment

Books authored: *How To Do Everything With Photoshop CS, Photoshop and Dreamweaver Integration, Photoshop CS for Digital Photographers*

Books co-authored: *How to Wow for the Web, Photoshop Most Wanted 1 and 2, New Masters Of Photoshop 1 and 2, Foundation Photoshop 6, Photoshop 7 Trade Secrets, From Photoshop to Dreamweaver*

Magazines written for: *Photoshop User, Mac Design, Computer Arts, Practical Web Projects, Web Designer, Digital Imaging*

Awards: Photoshop World Guru Award, First Place Illustration 2001; Photoshop World Guru Award, First Place Illustration 2002; Photoshop World Guru Award, Web Design 2002; MacWorld Digital Design; Dynamic Graphics (Recognition for outstanding Graphic Design); AIDA Graphex 33 Citation.

Web Sites: www.photoshopcafe.com, www.pixeloverload.com,

What type of work do you do?

I find myself working on anything from an HTML- or Flash-based site to digital illustration with Photoshop. Lately, I have been working more with the film and music industries where I blend photorealistic illustration with photos, video, and sound, and assemble the project in Flash.

What got you interested in this field?

As a kid, I enjoyed immersing myself in the arts, and I think that just lead to the computer and then to the commercial route.

What was your first industry-related job?

I was on staff at *Voice Magazine* and quickly became senior designer, then art director. I learned a lot because I was fortunate to work closely with Dr. Jerry Jenson, who had fifty years of experience. He taught me to look beyond the eye candy and inject meaning into my designs.

What type of hardware/software do you use?

I have four machines (Windows and Mac), but my workhorse is a dual 2 Ghz Mac G5. It has 2.5 GB of RAM, 160 GB and 200 GB hard drives, and a 160 GB Firewire drive for backups. I use a dual monitor setup with an Apple 20" Cinema (LCD) and Apple 21" (CRT) Studio Display. I also love my Wacom Intuos3 tablet and my Cambridge Soundworks Model Eleven satellite and sub system for music.

I use Adobe Creative Suite Pro and Macromedia Studio Pro software. The applications I use the most are Photoshop, Dreamweaver, Flash, Illustrator, InDesign, Final Cut HD, and Strata 3D CX.

This image of my guitar was created entirely in Photoshop. No scans, photos, third-party plugins, or 3D programs were used.

Where do you find creative inspiration?

Something happens while I am watching movies; I get the urge to create something. Sometimes I want to rush out of the theater and go directly to my computer. I also find a lot of inspiration in books and magazines. Music influences me; I listen to many styles of music, depending on the type of design I am working on.

What would you consider your biggest career accomplishment?

Building and running PhotoshopCAFE.com. I founded the CAFÉ in 2000 to give back to the design community. I display the work I do for fun and write free tutorials. I've been rewarded by meeting really cool people and feeling the heartbeat of the design community. The site has become the number one most visited Photoshop-related website on the Web. I plan to do a major redesign of the site since it still has my four-year-old design, but the content is always fresh.

I've also launched a series of training CDs on www.photoshopcd.com. I travel the country and teach seminars. I found out that I enjoy teaching others as much as I enjoy designing.

What types of credentials are most important in finding a job in your field?

Paper credentials don't mean as much to me as natural credentials. The important ones are talent, willingness and hunger to learn, and the desire to stretch and take risks. You need to be able to look at something that seems too big for you, and then jump in and finish it. You need to be willing to work long, hard hours and keep your focus through the whole process. Attention to detail and a desire to go the extra mile will not hurt, either.

What types of challenges do you face daily ?

Juggling all the work and deadlines. I work on multiple jobs at the same time and wear many hats. I can plan everything out and schedule all the work, and then something can come in with a tight deadline that sends a ripple effect through the whole scheduling process. In this business you have to be flexible and willing to work extra hours to manage everything and still meet all the deadlines. I have found that the best way to be prepared is by resisting the urge to procrastinate. Don't leave a job to the last moment, because you may not have that last moment free!

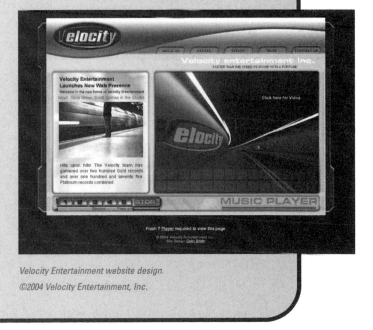

Velocity Entertainment website design.
©2004 Velocity Entertainment, Inc.

ANIMATION AND INTERACTIVITY

What better way to keep users interested in your site than to make them participants? Sites that respond to a user's input by doing more than just loading up a new page are much more exciting and interesting. Throughout this book, we've mentioned only general categories of software. This was intentional, since there are often a number of competing software packages that do the same thing, and what you use often depends on what your school, company, or client prefers. However, in the arena of website interactivity, there is one application that dwarfs all the rest: Macromedia Flash. There are a few other applications that do similar things, but Flash is used more often in the industry than anything else.

This interactive promotional CD was created in Flash for Culinard, the Culinary Institute of Virginia College *(www.culinard.com)* by Derek Mathews of Dragonfly Digital *(www. dragonfly3d.com)* and Jason Hutton *(www.jasonhutton.net)*. Among the many interactive components, including full-motion video and photo galleries, there is a 360-degree virtual tour.

By now I'm sure you've encountered a number of websites that require you to download the Flash Player. This is a free download from Macromedia that allows you to view content created in Flash. You may also notice that a lot of sites that include Flash content also provide an alternate standard version of the site. Flash is designed to be used by people with low as well as high bandwidth, so although the experience may be somewhat lessened by using a 56K modem, you should still be able to enjoy the site. However, there is another reason to provide a non-Flash version of your site: if users visit strictly to obtain information, they may not be interested in being wowed or entertained by your clever interactive animations. They may view them as a waste of time. While the majority of your users may love the Flash content, you should still provide alternatives to keep from alienating those who don't.

figure | 7-8 |

This animation by Jason Hutton
(www.jasonhutton.net)
demonstrates how Flash
can be used for character
lip sync.

Simple Versus Complex Animation

Animated GIFs were discussed briefly in an earlier chapter; they are mentioned again here to further explain the difference between an animated GIF and Flash animation. An animated GIF is nothing more than a series of still images strung together. These images are read by your browser and shown one at a time in a specific sequence. That's all. You can include things like transparency and instructions about how long to display each image, but that's about it. Flash is capable of producing enormously more complex animations. Comparing the two is like comparing a flip-book to an animated feature film.

Flash Intros and Loaders

Two common features of Flash sites are the intro and the loader. The intro is intended to be the hook that draws you into the site. It usually only lasts a few seconds, and should be quick, catchy, and interesting. It's a tiny commercial for the website, intended to give you an exaggerated taste of what you can expect on the inside, the same way a trailer for an upcoming feature film makes you want to stand in line for tickets. One important thing to realize, though, is that no matter how much you want to see the movie, by the fifteenth time you've seen the same trailer, you start to change the channel. Your Flash intro may be great, but no one wants to see it every time they visit your site. For this reason, it's common to include a small, unobtrusive link that allows the user to "skip intro." A small thing, but it goes a long way toward people wanting to come back to your site.

figure **7-9**

Flash can be used to create entire cartoons for viewing on or off the Web. Pictured here is *Fergy & Sizzle* by David San Miguel. ©2004 David San Miguel.

figure **7-10**

Flash animation doesn't have to be silly or funny, as demonstrated by *Dark Ronin: Chapter One* by Jake Shill. ©2004 Jake Shill.

Even though Flash content is relatively small, it can still take some time to load. Just because you're promising cool Flash content doesn't mean that users will suddenly become more patient. You still need to give them something to hold their interest during the download process. If your Flash content takes more than five or six seconds to download on a 56K modem, you probably need to include a loader. This can be something as simple as a little bar on the screen that shows the progress of the download. At least the users have something nice to look at and can tell that something is happening. If they see nothing but a blank screen, they have no idea if they'll have to wait three more seconds or six minutes. Some loaders take it a step further and include a slide show of images or even simple games to play while you wait. Unless you have something massive that takes a long while to download, the simple progress bar is just fine.

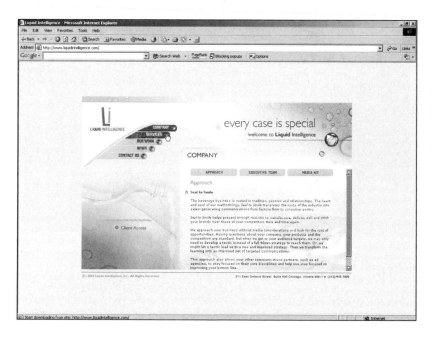

figure | 7-11 |

This site is LiquidIntelligence.com, developed by 2Advanced Studios, LLC. Notice how the graphics are very clean and professional. Although you can't tell in this still image, there is a constant, soothing motion of air bubbles rising in the upper right corner.

Flash Interfaces

Flash interfaces can vary widely. If you know how to use the application very well, you can make it do pretty much anything you want. Text, images, and shapes can fade in and out, change size, change color, change shape, move around, and do all kinds of other things—all in direct response to the user. Therein lies the success of Flash sites. They not only entertain, but also draw users in and make them feel like the interface is a customized machine, responding to them personally.

As cool as Flash is, you can also overdo it. Keep yourself in check. Make sure the transitions between the act of clicking a button and the result of clicking that button aren't too long. For example, if every time I click a button, a menu takes half a second to slide out and flash a different color, it keeps my interest. On the other hand, if every time I click a button, a robot arm comes out and spends six seconds assembling the new menu letter-by-letter, I'll probably get fed up and leave the site after the second click.

figure | 7-12 |

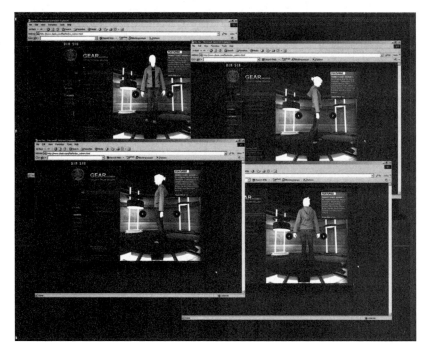

The Dia Sin Clothing site *(www.diasin.com)*, developed by 2Advanced Studios, LLC, uses interactive 3D rotations to demonstrate their clothing lines.

Flash Movies

Flash isn't only used for designing interactive interfaces; it can also be used to create animated movies. In fact, you can put the two together and create interactive animated movies, for example, a movie that includes buttons to let you determine the fate of a character. The possibilities are virtually limitless. All you have to do is perform an Internet search for "Flash animations" and you can be entertained for hours by the results. The software itself is fairly complicated, but there are tutorials and books available that can make it relatively easy to learn. It also pays to research traditional character animation techniques, since many of them can also be applied to Flash. Flash movies can be a big draw to your website, as long as they are relevant to what you're doing. For example, you wouldn't put an animated cartoon on a site for a financial institution, but you might for a skate supply store. Just like everything else, use it in moderation and only when appropriate, but Flash animation skills can be an important addition to your design palette.

figure 7-13

Humor and Kung-Fu fighting. They just never get old, as illustrated in this excellent Flash cartoon by A. Rhoades. ©2004 A. Rhoades.

INTERNET GAMING

Everybody likes games. Games entertain us and distract us from the daily grind. Immersive virtual reality games are even being developed now to distract children from the unpleasantness of a doctor's visit. "Sure, I'll get a shot if I can put on those goggles and play that cool skateboarding game!" Games attract users and keep their attention. They can lessen the pain of a long download time, or they can be the reason a person visits your site.

figure |7-14|

Flash Games

Flash games require a bit more knowledge and experience than creating an interactive interface or an animation. Flash includes its own programming language called ActionScript. It's not impossibly difficult as programming languages go, but it will require some research and study, as well as math.

Think you've seen every superhero under the sun? It's a bird. It's a plane. No, it's an invincible brick. From the mind of Jacob Swimmer, he comes to save us from monotony. ©2004 Jacob E. Swimmer.

figure |7-15|

If you're willing to spend some extra time learning to program and brush up on your math skills, you can create really cool Flash games like Jason Hutton. ©2004 Jason Hutton.

In general, Flash games are simple, but they can get complex if you're willing to spend the time programming them. If, on the other hand, you have no interest in learning programming of any kind, you severely limit yourself as a designer. Sooner or later, you'll encounter something a client wants that can only be done by coding it in a **scripting language**. It always pays to broaden your skill set.

Java Games

Java is a programming language that can also be used to create web-based computer games. It's by no means the only one available, nor does it only create programs for the Web, but its use on the Web is fairly common and so bears discussion. This is not to be confused with **JavaScript**, which is related but not as robust. JavaScript is a language used to perform functions within a web page. Programs written in JavaScript cannot stand alone. A Java program compiled (rewritten) for the Web, called an **applet**, is a standalone application. This requires some serious programming—not at all for the casual web designer, but again the more related skills you can incorporate into your toolset, the more marketable you become.

Gaming Servers

Multiplayer online games are a big commodity. There are many services on the Internet that allow you to connect and play games with people from all over the world. While you can do this with some of the simpler games we discussed earlier (for example, a digital chess game), the major 3D action or role-playing games require robust server machines to provide this kind of connectivity. They are mentioned here mainly to draw the distinction between this kind of online gaming and the simpler web-based applications we have previously discussed. Major multiplayer games are not something that can be incorporated into a website as a design element. Gaming sites that provide this kind of service do not require web developers to create their games. At least not for now. Keep an eye on the technology; maybe you'll be the one to find a way to incorporate a major multiplayer experience into a website interface.

figure |7-16|

What do you think constitutes a geek? Check out Derek Mathews's Build-a-Geek, constructed in Flash *(www.dragonfly3d.com)*. ©2004 Derek Mathews, Dragonfly Digital.

figure |7-17|

The infamous Doctor Duck, created and animated in Flash. ©2004 David San Miguel.

figure | 7-18 |

This is Neostream *(www.neostream.com)*. The little figure you see was created in 3D and incorporated into a Flash design. He is very interactive. You can slap him around with the mouse, and he reacts to it in different ways, depending on the speed and position of your strike.

3D ON THE WEB

Moving out of the realm of 3D games on the Web, we come now to 3D design elements. 3D modeling and animation is an extremely competitive field. It requires an enormous level of dedication and talent to master even one of the expansive software packages that enable you to model, texture, light, and animate three-dimensional elements. However, if you possess this skill, there are equally wonderful applications available that can translate that 3D animation into Flash. Beyond that, there are also applications that allow you to design 3D specifically for the Web. Using this technology can allow you to achieve results that just aren't possible with traditional Flash animation alone.

3D technology is here to stay. Recent big-budget films have proven to us that 3D graphics can be used to create photorealistic scenery, objects, and even characters that are indistinguishable from real life. It only makes sense that this technology would evolve to the Web. As time goes on, the two will become ever more integrated. Will you be the one to pioneer the next big form of 3D-Web integration?

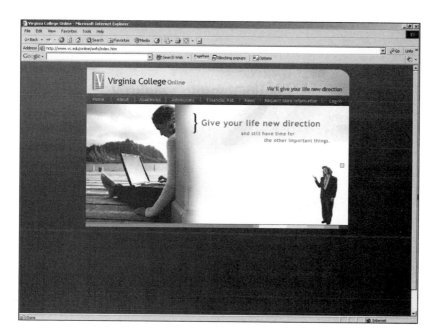

figure |7-19|

Virginia College Online features a miniature guide in full-motion video. That's her in the lower right corner. She appears on each page to give you a better explanation of the content (www.vconline.edu).

CHAPTER SUMMARY

So, where will this technology lead us? What will the Web look like in five years? In ten years? That all depends on how well future web designers can harness emerging technologies to channel their creative potential into the production of bold, new innovations. You now have some idea of what kinds of technological advancements have made the addition of multimedia to the Web possible. Stay on top of it and keep an open mind. Never limit yourself to the present. We have the technology now to transmit audio/visual signals at the speed of light without cables. We have the technology in place to take a three-dimensional computer model and turn it into a real object, made out of plastic or even metal. What else do you think we'll be able to do in the near future, and how can you make it work for the Web? As a web designer, this is your charge: push the envelope and find ways to give Web users what they want in ways they never expected.

in review

1. What is meant by the term multimedia?

2. How does a broadband Internet connection differ from a dial-up modem?

3. What are four types of broadband connections, and how do they compare?

4. What is a MIDI file, and why shouldn't you use it on the web?

5. What is streaming media?

6. What is Macromedia Flash?

7. What is the Flash Player?

8. What does it mean for a website to be interactive?

9. What good is a Flash intro, and why should you enable users to skip it?

10. What is a loader, and why should you use one?

11. As a web designer, why is it important to learn programming?

12. What are two tools you can use to create online games?

13. What does 3D have to do with the Web?

14. What can you imagine for the future of web design?

exercises

1. Think about all the technological innovations you've encountered in science fiction books and movies. How far in the future do you think wrist communicators and electronic paper are? Design a website that would work if a user was viewing it on a wrist communicator. Create this site in several stages representing how it would change interactively, and write a brief explanation of how these changes would occur.

2. Look at some interactive Flash sites on the Web and then sketch out a storyboard on paper of a Flash interface you'd like to create. This means sketch out your design in separate frames, as if you were drawing a comic book with multiple panels on each page. Let each frame represent a different stage of your interactive animation.

3. Sketch out an idea for a quick interactive game someone could play on your website. Nothing complex—make it simple, but interesting.

4. Write out a description of what you think it will be like to access the World Wide Web twenty years from now. You can write this as a straight-forward essay, or treat it as a creative writing assignment and write it as a short-story. Check out the Vodafone Future Vision Website (www.vodafone.com/futurevision) for inspiration.

glossary

analog: in general, a continuous signal, or a device that transmits or conducts a continuous signal. In reference to data transfer, an analog phone line is one that receives and conducts a continuous electrical signal from a modem or telephone. In contrast, a digital phone line transmits individual data packets without being converted into a continuous analog signal.

analogous: a color scheme with three to five colors that are next to each other on the color wheel.

applet: a program that is designed to run from within another application, as opposed to a standalone application.

ascenders: the parts of a font that go above the x-height line.

banding: a harsh transition between colors, which is the result of the limited number of colors available in a GIF format. The resulting transition looks like bands of color.

bandwidth: transfer speed, or the amount of data that can be transmitted in a specified length of time, usually measured in kilobits per second (Kbps) or megabits per second (Mbps).

baseline: the invisible line on which the base, or the bottom, of a letter is aligned.

bit: a binary number, either 1 or 0.

broadband: a medium which allows multiple data signals to be transmitted at once, increasing the speed of transmission.

byte: a group of eight bits.

cache: in general, a device or specified location set aside for high-speed storage and retrieval of data. In reference to the Web, it is a section of the hard drive designated to store images downloaded from a web page. The next time that page is visited, those images can be called up quickly from the hard drive, rather than waiting for them to be downloaded again.

complementary: a color scheme using complementary colors, which are the colors opposite one another on the color wheel.

compression: reducing the amount of data in a file, so that it takes up less storage space. There are different methods of compression. See *lossless compression* and *lossy compression*.

creative process: a personalized system of approaching a design project, intended to stimulate the creative faculties.

CSS (Cascading Style Sheets): a feature added to websites that gives web designers and users more control over how pages are displayed.

demographics: the characteristics of human populations and population segments, especially when used to identify web audiences.

dithering: creating the illusion of new colors and shades by varying the combination of pixels.

double contrast: a color scheme using the colors on either side of the chosen complementary colors.

drop-down navigation: a menu system that initially displays only major topics; once a major topic is clicked, a list of related subtopics appears underneath it. Also called pull-down navigation.

font: a complete assortment of symbols and characters, with a distinctive design.

font family: a group of variations on a single font.

GIF (Graphics Interchange Format): web-based image format that supports 256 colors, transparency, and animations.

grayscale: a design scheme that uses only black, white, and shades of gray.

hexadecimal: a number and letter system that is used to translate colors into a code that computers can understand.

image compression: see *compression*.

intermediate colors: the colors on the color wheel that are created by combining primary and secondary colors.

JavaScript: a scripting language based on Java, but developed independently; it allows dynamic content to be added to web pages.

JPEG (Joint Photographic Experts Group): image format that supports up to 16.7 million colors, and uses lossy compression to permit a smaller file size.

kerning: the space between individual letters.

kilobit (Kb): actually 1,024 bits, but often rounded off to 1,000 bits.

kilobits per second (Kbps): a measure of bandwidth or transfer speed; the number of kilobits transferred in one second.

kilobyte (KB): actually 1,024 bytes, but often rounded off to 1,000 bytes.

leading: the vertical space between two lines of type.

loader: a small animation used to let a visitor know how much of a site has loaded on a fully animated site.

lossless compression: a type of compression used in GIF images, in which all the image data is left intact.

lossy compression: a type of compression used in JPEG images, in which some of the image data is permanently removed.

monochromatic: a color scheme using only one color and its tints and shades.

multimedia: presentation that integrates some combination of text, video, sound, graphics, and animation.

navigation: the way menu links are structured; the way to travel from one page to the next, and back again.

pixels: small squares of color that are used to make up raster images viewed on a computer.

PNG (Portable Network Graphics): web-based image format that is similar to GIF, but is patent-free.

primary colors: the three colors that are the foundation of the color wheel, and from which all other colors are made: red, yellow, and blue.

raster image: images created from a collection of pixels; also known as bitmapped images.

red-green color blindness: the most common type of color blindness, the result of an inability to distinguish between red and green.

resolution: the number of pixels per square inch that an image inhabits; 72 pixels per inch is the standard size for images on the Web.

resolution independent: images that rely on mathematical points rather than pixels, which can be resized without affecting quality. See *vector image*.

RGB color model: the default computer color model, which creates color by using red, green, and blue.

RYB color model: the color model which uses red, yellow, and blue pigment to create all other colors.

sans serif: fonts without decorative strokes.

saturation: the level of a color's vividness or dullness.

scale: a method for resetting the height and width of your text.

scope: a statement of precisely what you plan to do for a client and at what price.

scripts: programs that are designed to be executed without explicit user interaction.

scripting language: a code that is used to program scripts. See *scripts*.

secondary colors: the three colors that are created by combining two of the primary colors: purple, green, and orange.

serif: fonts with decorative strokes.

shades: darker values of a color.

site map: visual map of the site's navigation.

split complementary: color scheme using a color in combination with the two colors directly to the left and right of its complement.

style sheets: see *CSS*.

theme: a recurrent idea expressed through the use of related concepts in a design.

tints: lighter values of a color.

tracking: the spacing between all letters in a line.

triadic: color scheme using three colors that are equal distances apart on the color wheel.

typography: the art of manipulation of text on the page.

value: the amount of lightness in a color, expressed through tint and shade.

vector image: a resolution-independent image created by connecting lines between plotted mathematical points.

web-safe color palette: a set of 216 colors that can be viewed on almost any color monitor, and interpreted by any web browser.

white space: the space on a web page in which no design elements are used.

x-height: the height of the lowercase letter *x*.

index